A 30-DAY GUIDE TO A DYNAMIC PRAYER LIFE

LEARNING TO PRAY LIKE JESUS

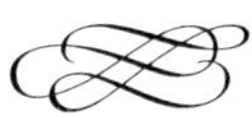

REV. DR. DIEUNER JOSEPH

May God use these lessons to help your prayer life growth stronger and deeper.

COPYRIGHT

Published Internationally by Dieuner Joseph
North Carolina USA
www.disciplemakerministry.com

ISBN 978-0-578-24139-5

Virginia Phillips-Hall

CONTENTS

PREFACE

I have been pastoring for the past twenty-six years. Ironically, I have found a unique challenge in the church: trying to lead (or convince) God's people to invest in a lifestyle of earnest prayer. You would think this would not be true of people who spend a lot of time in church. But we are busy people, and our churches are busy places. Getting church people to pray earnestly and effectually is no easy task.

I will admit for my first ten years as a pastor, I did not fully understand the depth of prayer that God (and life) requires of us. Prayer is the most fundamental calling of every believer. God's voice calls us to seek Him and prayer is our employ. It is the occupation of which we are to occupy ourselves.

This book written by Dr. Dieuner Joseph is a challenge to all of us. It is a challenge to respond to God's calling to a life of consistent prayer and consecration. We need to be challenged. Without challenges we settle for mediocrity.

I have known Dieuner Joseph for three decades. He is a man of great learning and a skilled writer. Far more significantly, I know him to be a man of prayer. He is a man of passionate prayer. The words in this devotional are not written simply from the vantage of a scholar, but from his own personal triumphs and struggles in prayer. Dieuner

Joseph has spent decades of countless hours wrestling in prayer at the altar, engaging in all night sessions, prayer retreats, and seasons of fasting – a lifestyle of prayer. The content in this book is born from the laboratory of life. He is a pastor who has dedicated years discipling God's people in the practice of prayer.

There are some things about prayer we can only learn on our knees. The most effective way for each reader to benefit from this book is to couple it with the daily discipline of prayer. Prayer is an experience that transforms our hearts and renews our minds by exposing our souls to the shining light of God's presence. By following the Biblically based prescriptions in this book, may we all find the everlasting peace and joy prayer produces.

Rev. Eric M, Beckham
Sr. Pastor, Zion Baptist Church
Marietta, Georgia

INTRODUCTION

In August 2019, while on a Caribbean cruise with my family, the Holy Spirit told me to go to a private area on the cruise ship so He could speak with me. It was 6:00 a.m. While sitting and contemplating the beauty of the ocean as the ship sailed through the sea, the Holy Spirit told me to write down the chapters for this book. Since I did not have a pen handy, I used an app on my cell phone to write down everything the Holy Spirit told me to write. When the Spirit was done, I was totally speechless and confounded. I rushed back to my cabin, jumped on my computer, wrote everything down and then saved it, in case something happened with my phone.

Every believer is a student in the school of prayer. None of us can claim mastery of the prayer exercise. Because prayer is a learned spiritual language, it takes time to develop the aptitude to pray effectually. The time we invest to become more fluent in the language of prayer is certainly not wasted. It is a spiritual investment with many benefits for our spiritual growth.

Our spiritual growth is not ours alone. It is for the advancement of the kingdom of God on earth and profitable for loved-ones and members of the body of Christ. Such growth is certainly built on the foundation of prayer. Prayer is one of the most essential spiritual disciplines believers cannot do without. Unfortunately, many believers struggle in their prayer life because they do not know the fundamentals of prayer and how those fundamentals can be practiced. Like all other spiritual disciplines, becoming fluent in the language of prayer takes time and training. Having a prayer mentor is paramount for everyone who desires to develop a fervent and effectual prayer life.

To pastors, small group facilitators and Bible Study teachers, as the facilitators or instructors of this book, you play an important role in helping to shape the way people in your spiritual context feel about prayer and how they pray. This is an enormous responsibility that must not be taken lightly. One reason you have been tasked with the responsibility to teach the lessons in this book is because of your passion for prayer, or because you have demonstrated a level of spiritual maturity that makes you a credible spiritual leader. However, unto whom much is given, much is required (Luke 12:48) [1].

What is required of every instructor or facilitator of this book is preparation, inspiration, and dedication. Preparation is something you control. Take the time to read the book and the scripture references. Familiarize yourself with the self-reflection questions, as well as, the questions for small group discussion. Think of creative ways to teach each session. Read commentaries and other resources to strengthen your understanding of the primary texts in each section. Do not hesitate to consult other instructors and share teaching tips. Remember, knowledge is power. The more you prepare, the more you will know. The more you know, the more you will be able to share with students how to become more fervent and effectual in prayer.

Inspiration comes from the Holy Spirit. However, any inspiration absent of preparation leads to speculation instead of edification. In other words, we have to give God something to work with. The Almighty God can take our feeble preparation and turn it into a masterful tool of edification. He can inspire you to meet your students where they are so they can become more confident in the ministry of prayer. However, you must become a student of prayer before you can inspire others as a prayer-mentor. This means you have to allow the Holy Spirit to saturate your soul through prayer so you can become an agent of prayer. Then you will develop the relevant vocabulary to teach others about prayer.

Dedication to the word of God, to a life of prayer and to those you mentor in your spiritual context will endear you to them and give you the credibility to share the knowledge you have gained through this book with authenticity and boldness. The book contains 30 daily lessons with two bonus lessons to which you must dedicate preparation and prayer, time along with encouraging the students to grow deeper and wiser in the ministry of prayer. Students will benefit from your ongoing outreach through social media and other platforms to keep them informed and engaged. Pray for God to give you courage to resist any desire to quit on the class, or not to spend enough time to cultivate your own prayer life.

In the end, your teaching is only as good as the life of prayer you nurture. After all, no one can lead where they have never been. Students are eager to be led into a prayer adventure. Think of yourself as a tour guide. Your role is to guide students in their prayer journey. You are a spiritual resource well students will draw wisdom from to learn more about prayer. This well of information can only remain full through your own fervent prayer life. Make the adventure as enjoyable for the students as it is for you. Prayer should be a dynamic and exciting spiritual exercise. After all, what can be more exciting than engaging our Heavenly Father in a conversation through prayer?

This book on prayer is designed as a devotional/study guide to allow individuals and small groups to expand their biblical understanding and practice of prayer. This author assumes we are all deficient in the ministry of prayer. I have invested decades in learning to pray fervently and effectually. Yet, I often find myself struggling to go to the next level in my prayer life. During my conversation with the Holy Spirit on the cruise ship, I was made aware of the many mistakes I make when I prayed. Thus, I started the book by highlighting what prayer is not.

After establishing what prayer is not, I highlight in Chapter II the eight major characteristics of prayer to give a Bible-based blueprint of what praying to God should look and sound like. In Chapter III, I discuss the purpose of prayer. People need to know why they pray, and why prayer is such a fundamental spiritual discipline. In Chapter IV, I focus on the power of prayer. Believers should know that prayer is a potent spiritual weapon given to them by God to live victoriously through Christ Jesus. In the final chapter, I review the different types of prayer common in the Christian Church. I want believers to learn about the specificity of prayer and the language they should use when communicating with God about different needs.

I want to extend my sincere gratitude to my beloved wife Colette and my daughter Lysandra for helping to edit the book. Their feedback was invaluable. They helped me remain practical and plain in my theological discourse. I also owe a debt of gratitude to my prayer partner and long-time friend, Pastor Eric M. Beckham whose wisdom, support and comments helped to make the book a practical guide that can be used to strengthen the prayer ministry in any Christian Church.

To everyone using this valuable teaching resource, watch how your life will be transformed by your willingness and dedication to be a prayer warrior or a prayer-mentor. Then be prepared for a powerful move of God as you let the Lord use you to the utmost. Know the time you spend in preparation, meditation and consecration will not be in vain.

---

1. This book uses the New International Version (NIV) as its primary biblical source. Wherever the NIV is not used, the version is explicitly mentioned.

DEDICATION

This book is dedicated to my late mother, Lucienne Joseph, who was a prayer warrior and a devoted disciple of Jesus Christ. It is because of her commitment to prayer that I have become a dedicated student in the school of prayer.

CHAPTER I

WHAT PRAYER IS NOT

What causes fights and quarrels among you? Don't they come from your desires that battle within you? You desire but do not have, so you kill. You covet but you cannot get what you want, so you quarrel and fight. You do not have because you do not ask God. When you ask, you do not receive, because you ask with wrong motives, that you may spend what you get on your pleasures. James 4:1-3

Humanity has an innate desire to communicate with its creator. That desire was amplified after we were evicted from the Garden of Eden, following the sin of Adam and Eve. Our communication with our creator is called prayer.

Prayer is one of the most important theological topics in the Christian Bible. Followers of God have been praying for thousands of years. Yet prayer remains one of the most misunderstood spiritual exercises. Countless books, articles, journals, and curriculum have been written about prayer. Numerous sermons have been preached about the necessity of prayer for spiritual growth. Nevertheless, a majority of Christians struggle to maintain a dynamic prayer life. Perhaps it is because we do not know what prayer is, though we assume we do.

Prayer is often thought of as an activity whereby the supplicant presents his or her request to the Lord through a verbal petition. It is regularly practiced as a unidirectional exercise as opposed to a two-way interaction. Often the petitioner begins with words of gratitude and jumps right into their petition. It is usually transactional as we often aim to get something from the divine.

For thousands of years, people had prayed in the Old Testament. Nevertheless, Jesus felt it necessary to take the time to teach his disciples to pray (Luke 11:1-11). Jesus taught extensively about prayer throughout his ministry. He chastised the Pharisees for not knowing how to pray. He criticized the arrogance of the religious leaders of his day for their hypocrisy in praying to be recognized for their piety.

There are 21 passages in the New Testament that capture Jesus' teaching on prayer. He also told two parables about prayer (Luke 18:1–14). Jesus not only taught about prayer, he had a dynamic and consistent personal prayer life, though he did not need any material blessings from the Father. During his three years of ministry, the Bible records Jesus praying 25 different times.

Many people do not pray because they think prayer is a wasteful exercise. More often than not, these are individuals whose prayers were not answered for one reason or another. The distrust in prayer is often the result of one's misunderstandings about prayer. I believe the more we understand the spiritual exercise of prayer, the more apt we are to pray.

How do people learn about the exercise of prayer? Unfortunately, there is no school that can teach one to pray fervently and effectually. Even a seminary degree on the spiritual practice of prayer does not guarantee that one will master the art of prayer. Indeed, I do not think the spiritual exercise of prayer can ever be mastered. After all, notwithstanding our spiritual maturity, we still do not pray as we should. Thus, the Holy Spirit makes intercession for us with *unspoken groaning* (Romans 8:26).

The Bible provides extensive instructions about prayer. However, prayer is not solely a Christian practice. Non-Christians pray, as well as followers of other religions. Muslims, for example, are required to pray five times per day, as prayer is one of the five pillars of Islam.

Some schools of Buddhism use meditational chanting as a form of prayer. The Hindu devotional Bhakti movements emphasize repetitive prayer.

Throughout my pastorate, I have seen people using different approaches in prayer to get a favorable response from the Almighty. Some people beg God to answer the prayers in times of distress, while others try to negotiate with the Almighty. There are those who even try to bribe God to answer their prayers. Many people even threatened God if He does not answer their prayer, as if God needs some type of favor from them.

All these misinformed approaches to prayer are evident in the Old Testament. Here again, I think that is why Jesus had to teach His disciples and the rest of his followers how to pray. What we learn from Jesus is that prayer is both a simple spiritual exercise and a complex ritual that requires thoughtful planning and intentionality. Before we can talk about the characteristics of prayer, I think it is beneficial to talk about what prayer is not.

DAY 1

PRAYER IS NOT BEGGING

God does not need us to beg Him to answer our prayers. After all, God promised to *supply all our needs according to His riches in glory* (Philippians 4:19). God knows everything we are going to say before we even say it. Begging implies an attempt to force God to do something He can do but is reluctant to do. This would suggest God is whimsical and temperamental.

God wants us to ask, and not beg. He asks us to trust His providential love and depend on His unfailing grace. God is a loving Father who does not need his children to beg for His divine favor and mercy. My children do not have to beg me to take them to the doctor when they are sick. They do not have to beg for food when they are hungry. Nor do they have to beg me to keep them safe from strangers. I do these things for them automatically, whether they are obedient or not, because that is what a good father does.

The Bible also describes God as a friend who sticks closer than a brother (Proverbs 18:24). A good friend does not have to beg another friend in time of need. Begging indicates a lack of intimacy. However, as redeemed servants of Jesus Christ, we have a relationship of loving union with the Father. His eyes are on the righteous, and His ears are attentive to His servants cry (Psalm 34:15).

The Lord hides us in His secret place (Psalm 91:1) to keep us safe from the attacks of the enemy. Therefore, there is no need to beg. All we have to do is cry out to Him and He will deliver us from our troubles (Psalm 34:17). Indeed, the Lord invites us to come boldly to His throne of grace, that we may obtain mercy and find grace to help us in time of need (Hebrews 4:16).

So then, God does not expect us to use our intimate time of prayer as an opportunity to beg. The soul that begs is a soul that lives in hopelessness and fear. The spirit of begging is an anti-Christ spirit that thinks it can manipulate the Almighty to do what He does not want to do. It is a spirit of deception seeking to turn prayer from a spiritual conversation into a personal transaction.

Besides, God does not respond to begging. He responds to petitions, intercessions, and invocation. Can you imagine having a friend who only communicates with you to beg for things he or she needs? Begging not only removes the spiritual intimacy from our communication with God, but it also dishonors the providential love of God.

When David begged God to spare the child who was conceived in his illicit relationship with Bathsheba, God did not honor his begging (2 Samuel 12:16); the child died anyway. Begging does not impress God or make Him act any faster. God is not moved by begging. He is moved by faith. In James 1:6, we are told we should make our petitions to God with faith, without any doubting.

In Genesis 18:16–27, Abraham pleaded with God and tried to bargain with the Almighty not to destroy the people of Sodom, where his nephew Lot lived. This was the first notable prayer mentioned in the Bible. Yet, Sodom was destroyed by God because of the wickedness of its inhabitants. Sodom was a city destined to be consumed by the just wrath of God. Abraham's relationship with God and his incessant plea for mercy were not going to prevent God from destroying that sinful city.

Begging is doubting God will answer our petitions. It is an attempt to manipulate God because one does not believe God will do what is being asked. Seeking God and crying out for Him to work in our life is different from begging. Fervency in prayer comes from a place of faith. That type of faith is the opposite of begging.

QUESTIONS FOR PERSONAL REFLECTION

PRAYER IS NOT BEGGING

(Philippians 4:19)

Why do we not need to beg God when we pray?

God Said He would supply all of needs according to His riches in glory

What is an alternative to begging when communicating with God?

Ask in faith as the righteousness of God

Begging is a sign of hopelessness and fear.

What happened when David begged God for the life of his child with Bathsheba? (2 Samuel 12:16)

God did not honor David's pray and his son died

Why do you think God did not honor Abraham's plea on behalf of Sodom? (Genesis 18:16-27)

It was destroyed because of the wickedness of it's inhabitants

Why do you think God does not respond to begging?

God already knows what we have need of, we only have to ask according to His directive, not beg.

DAY 2

PRAYER IS NOT MAKING A DEAL WITH GOD

Have you ever tried to make a deal with God in prayer? I have. I can tell you God does not make deals. He does not need to make deals with anyone. God only answers prayers according to His will, and not according to our carefully packaged proposal.

What can anyone offer God that He does not already have? The world, and everything in it, belongs to Him. God is All-Sufficient, All-Knowing, and All-Powerful. He has no equal and no competitor. He stands above all things; He can change anything, and He can do anything.

In 1 Samuel 1:9-28, we are told the story of Hannah who prayed to God for a son. In verse 11, she made the following vow:

> *O Lord of Heaven's Armies, if you will look upon my sorrow and answer my prayer and give me a son, then I will give him back to you. He will be yours for his entire lifetime, and as a sign that he has been dedicated to the Lord, his hair will never be cut.*

Let us not forget Hannah had been going up to Shiloh year after year to offer the same deal, making her prayer to God to no avail.

However, just one prayer of intercession from the prophet Eli led to her prayer being answered. The characteristics of Eli's prayer demonstrate the reason it was so effective. **First**, it was based on faith. **Second**, it reflected Eli's friendship with God. **Third**, it assumed God had the power to do what was asked. **Fourth**, it affirmed the sovereignty of God to do what He wants when He wants.

It wasn't Hannah's deal-making ability that caused God to give her a son. Rather, it was the intercession of the prophet Eli on her behalf that led to her prayer being answered. Eli had such a relationship with God he did not have to beg on behalf of Hannah. In verse 17, Eli says, *Go in peace, and may the God of Israel grant you what you have asked of Him.* This suggests that Eli had total confidence in God. He told Hannah to go in peace. It is this type of faith that moves God to act.

When the prophet Isaiah was sent by God to tell Hezekiah he would die, Hezekiah did not try to negotiate with God (2 Kings 20:1–11). He did not say, "If you spare my life, or add more years to my life, I will do x, y, or z." He just prayed for the Lord's mercy based on his relationship and faithfulness to God. Within minutes, God answered his prayer.

Lastly, in Judges 11:30–31, Jephthah made an unnecessary vow to the Lord saying, *If you give the Ammonites into my hands, whatever comes out of the door of my house to meet me when I return in triumph from the Ammonites will be the LORD's, and I will sacrifice it as a burnt offering*. This was not necessary. He did not have to pray that quid pro quo prayer. God had already decided to deliver the Israelites from the Ammonites after the Israelites repented from their idolatrous ways in Judges 10:15–16.

All Jephthah needed to do was to march against the Ammonites to deliver his people. Because of this, he offered his only daughter as a sacrificial offering to God for the victory already guaranteed by God. Besides, human sacrifice was already banned by the Lord in Deuteronomy 18:10 (also Leviticus 18:21). The victory was the result of God's covenantal promise to Abraham, and not Jephthah's vow.

QUESTIONS FOR PERSONAL REFLECTION

PRAYER IS NOT MAKING A DEAL WITH GOD

(1 Samuel 1:9-28)

Why does it not make sense to try to make deals with God in prayer?

God is Soverign and can do what He wants when He wants Only answers prayer according to His will.

Why do you think God honored the prayer of Hannah, if He does not make any deal?

He answered because of the prayer of intercession made on her behalf by Prophet Eli

What lesson can be learned from Hezekiah about the way we should pray?

He had an intimate relationship with God and had faith and confidence that God would answer, so we must do same.

Who is Jephthah and what mistake did he make when he prayed for God to give the Ammonites into his hands?

His mistake was not knowing the will/word of God, that God did not accept human Sacrifice and that the people of had repented so He had already forgiven

Why should we not make promises to God when we pray?

We can't Offer God anything that He doesn't already have, it all belongs to Him already!

DAY 3

PRAYER IS NOT TELLING GOD SOMETHING HE DOES NOT ALREADY KNOW

God is All-Knowing. His knowledge is All-Encompassing. He knows the past, the present, and the future. He is the inventor of knowledge. God knows our thoughts before we think of them. He knows us better than we know ourselves. Thus, He has carefully customized our destiny and designed the trajectory of our lives before we were born.

There is not a thing we can say that God does not already know. God can discern our motives and can see the end at the same time as the beginning. We cannot teach God anything new. He is the authenticator of all revelations. Every idea comes from Him. He programmed the human brain to think, and knows every thought it contains. Thus, David said in Psalm 139:1–5:

You have searched me, LORD, and you know me.
You know when I sit and when I rise; you perceive my thoughts from afar.
You discern my going out and my lying down; you are familiar with all my ways.
Before a word is on my tongue you, LORD, know it completely.

If God already knows what we are going to say, if He already knows our thoughts, why then do we pray? God invites us to pray so we can fellowship with Him to revitalize our souls. Prayer is not intended to give God insights about our circumstances. God does not need us to tell Him when we are hungry, or discouraged, or hurting, or unemployed, or sick, or depressed, or in crises. Talking about our existential crises in prayer is a form of self-therapy. It is not meant to educate God about our circumstances. He already knows.

When a couple goes to therapy, they are encouraged to discuss the conflict in their marriage. Therapists are trained professionals. Their goal is to help patients make decisions and clarify their feelings in order to solve problems. Therapists provide support and guidance while helping patients make effective decisions within the overall structure of support. Most therapists have perfected the art of listening, so they can better help their patients. They are accustomed to hearing similar types of issues, complaints, and crises. Yet, they give each patient their undivided attention no matter how repetitive the patient may be.

God is the ultimate therapist. He allows us to express our crises, complaints, and issues in prayer as a way to provide support and guidance while helping us make spirit-led decisions within the overall structure of His providential love. He is not caught off guard by anything that proceeds from our mouths, nor is He waiting for us to tell Him about the happenings of our lives in our prayers. That is why we can pray without uttering a word from our lips. This does not mean we should not tell God everything we want to say to Him in our prayers. Remember, God is a loving Father and therapist, who invites us to share our life issues with Him. In Matthew 11:28, the Lord invites us to come to Him when we are weary and burdened so He can give us rest.

The outcome of our prayers is not determined by how much we say but by the intercession of the Holy Spirit. Prayer does not move God to do anything that was not part of His divine plan and according to His divine will. Prayer changes the petitioner, not the God, who hears our petition.

QUESTIONS FOR PERSONAL REFLECTION

PRAYER IS NOT TELLING GOD SOMETHING HE DOES NOT ALREADY KNOW

(Psalm 139:1-5)

Why is prayer not an information session for God?

God knows the past, present
and future of all.

If God already knows what we are going to say, why should we pray?

So we can fellowship with Him
and revitalize our souls

What did David say about God in Psalm 139:1-5, and how should that influence our prayer life?

David said in essence that God knows
everything there is to know about us

How does prayer function as spiritual therapy for believers?

It helps us to make Spirit led decisions

Why is the quantity of our spoken words not as significant as the disposition of our hearts when we pray?

God Knows our hearts and what we need even before we ask but as a father He wants us to petition Him! Then the Holy Spirit intercedes on our behalf.

DAY 4

PRAYER IS NOT AN ACT OF DESPERATION

Because God knows everything, He can do anything. We do not have to be desperate when we pray. Merriam-Webster Dictionary defines desperation as "the loss of hope and surrender to despair. It is a state of hopelessness leading to rashness." We should pray with faith, not desperation. For, *faith is confidence in what we hope for and assurance about what we do not see* (Hebrews 11:1).

Non-believers pray out of desperation because they do not have a relationship with God through Jesus Christ. Only in times of crises do they engage the Lord in a conversation for the sole purpose of asking for relief. Their prayers are always transactional because they come from a place of desperation.

A desperate person would talk to any deity. Such a person would not hesitate to go to a medium or a palm/card reader for answers—though these are forms of witchcraft forbidden by the God of the Bible. Some people go to voodoo priests when they are in desperate need of healing, money, or protection from demonic spirits. They just want a desired end, no matter what they have to do to get it. Their desperation makes them susceptible to spiritual deception of the enemy.

However, believers understand their lives are in the hands of the God who saved them and provided for their needs according to His riches in glory. Therefore, though they *are hard-pressed on every side, they are not crushed—perplexed, but not in despair* (2 Corinthians 4:8). God promises to give us strength in our weakness. Notwithstanding the extent of our existential crises, we have to remain hopeful.

Prayers of lament should not be confused with prayers of desperation. A prayer of lament is a prayer for help from God coming out of pain. Prayers of lament are the believer's way of crying out to God when they are overcome by the presence of chaos, brokenness, suffering, disaster, or death. It is a frank conversation, devoid of platitudes, wherein the petitioner expresses their afflictions to God. Those conversations can, at times, be blunt and angry. However, they are not irreverent.

One of the key differentiations between lament and desperation is prayers of lament capture the believer's determination to communicate with God in the depth of their pain. Prayers of lament are prayers of faith. It takes faith to call out to God in our brokenness, trusting that He hears us and will answer us. Prayers of lament are intensely emotional in nature because they originate from the depth of a wounded soul. On the other hand, most people lament their situation to the people in whom they confide and who care enough to listen. Desperate people will talk to anyone they think can help them. It is okay for us to lament our circumstance to God because He is our Father in heaven, who cares for us.

Only those in a relationship with God can send forth a prayer of lament. God is particularly sensitive to the cry of those who revere Him. He is loving enough to accept our anger and give us His sustaining grace in the midst of our adversity. Therefore, we do not have to pray in desperation.

QUESTIONS FOR PERSONAL REFLECTION

PRAYER IS NOT AN ACT OF DESPERATION

(2 Corinthians 4:8, Hebrews 11:1)

Why should Christians not pray out of desperation?

God already Knows all and can do anything

What is the difference between a prayer of lament and a prayer of desperation?

Prayer of lament is Cryin out to God for help in depth of pain or hurt. Desperation prayer is one of non believers they will pray to and deity, just wanting a desired end.

What is the danger of praying out of desperation?

you make yourself susceptible to spiritual deception of the enemy

What should you do when you are desperate to hear from God?

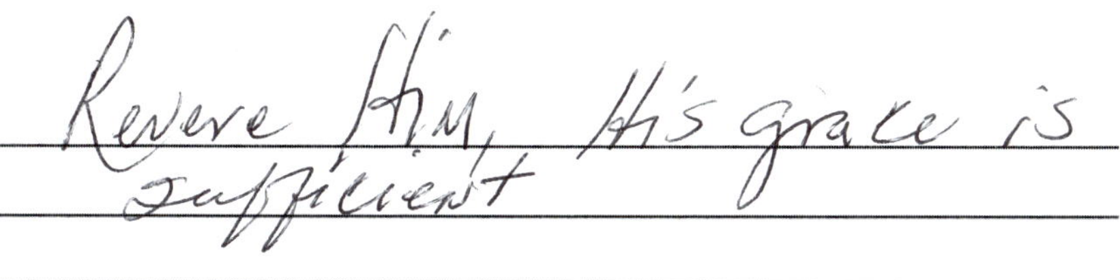

Praying out of desperation is a form of forbidden prayer to God and makes us susceptible to Spiritual deception of the enemy.

DAY 5

PRAYER IS NOT A DOCTORAL DISSERTATION

Years ago, I was invited to preach a revival in Tennessee. During the Sunday morning worship, one of the associate ministers was asked to do the altar prayer. The brother prayed for 45 minutes, nonstop. He prayed so long that people started to go back to their seats while he was praying. The people could not leave because I hadn't preached yet. If this had happened after the sermon, I have no doubt most people would have left. After the Service, I was told this individual is notorious for praying extensive prayers.

The effectiveness of our prayer is not determined by its length or theological complexity. God does not want us to recite a doctoral dissertation when we pray. In Matthew 6:7-8, Jesus said,

And when you pray, do not keep on babbling like pagans,
for they think they will be heard because of their many words.
Do not be like them, for your Father knows what you need
before you ask him.

A prayer does not have to be long and doctrinally sound to be effectual. A short and simple prayer can be as effective as a long prayer. It is not the number of words that matter. Rather, it is the condition of the heart.

There are times when all a believer need to say is "God, please help me." That is as powerful as any other prayer. The Lord's Prayer in the King James Version contains 66 words, 53 in the NIV. That is relatively short, and very precise. Yet, it remains the best prayer ever crafted.

Some of the most spiritually intense conversation and interaction with God is through meditation. The Holy Spirit intercedes for us through wordless groans. (Romans 8:26) People who are unable to speak can still pray effectually.

I know many people in my church who feel inadequate because they struggle to pray longer than five minutes. Some people refuse to join a prayer ministry or prayer team because they do not have too much to say in prayer. Others do not like to pray in public because they assume people will look down on their Christian faith since they cannot pray elaborately.

Though I am a writer, there are times when I am unable to say much when I pray. Sometimes, brevity is the manifestation of spiritual maturity. Besides, there are times when we have to be still before the Lord so we can hear Him talk to us. Indeed, there are times when the purpose of prayer is to hear from God, and not to say anything to Him.

My teenage son's prayer is no more than a few words. 30 seconds long. I sometimes think God listens to his prayer more than He listens to mine. Whenever we do family devotion, I look forward to hearing his 30 seconds prayer. Later on in life, his prayer will get longer as he experiences life's issues. However, for now, he is content to tell God just enough.

We should not allow anyone to pressure us into praying prolonged prayers. Prayer is an intimate language with which the believer communicates with God. It takes time to learn and master that language. Our prayer is a reflection of where we are in our spiritual journey. We cannot expect everyone to pray the same. The Almighty God does not! Therefore, you have to relax and enjoy the experience of prayer. God wants us to have delight in our conversation with Him.

QUESTIONS FOR PERSONAL REFLECTION

PRAYER IS NOT A DOCTORAL DISSERTATION

(Matthew 6:7-8)

What factors determine the effectiveness of prayer?

The condition of the heart
Spending time with God in prayer
Hear from God

Why did Jesus caution his disciples against babbling like pagans when they pray?

This was because the disciples thought
their prayers would be answered if
they prayed for a long time

What is the difference between a one-minute prayer and an hour prayer?

There is no difference, both
can be effective

What is the longest you ever prayed? How long do you pray on average?

I have prayed for an hour.
Now I average less than a minute
or sometimes 3-5 minutes when
spending time in prayer/meditation.

Do you think people who pray long prayers are more spiritually mature than others? Why?

No because the bible makes it
clear that both can be effective
It's about the condition of the heart

DAY 6

PRAYER IS NOT FORCING GOD'S HAND

God does not want us to feel pressured when we pray. He also does not want us to think we can pressure him in our prayers. When my mother was dying of liver cancer, I tried to pressure God to heal her right away. Of course, he did not. She went home to be with the Lord notwithstanding my pressured prayers.

No one can force God to act. All we can ask is for His will be done. Sometimes it is His will to heal and perform miracles. However, there are times when it is His will for our loved ones to return to their maker and have eternal rest from the vicissitudes of life. That does not mean God does not care or that He cannot do the impossible.

Here, again we have to remember prayer is a language of spiritual romance. It is a language of intimacy. There is no coercion in intimacy. God graciously and lovingly offered His Only Begotten Son as propitiation for the sins of humanity. Through Christ, He invites us into a relationship of loving union with him. He does not owe us anything. Therefore, He does not have to prove anything.

God is Self-Sustaining. He has no weakness, and does not need anything or anyone. Not even the devil can force God's hand. So, we should not assume we can pray in such a way as to force God to do something.

No one has the standing to make any demands on God. It is not because of our prayer God moves. He moves because of His love for us. God listens to us because He cares about us. The idea we can force Him to answer our prayer is preposterous. God's response to our prayer is a product of His faithfulness.

One of the passages often used to substantiate the idea we can force God's hand is Genesis 32:22-31. In it, we read the story of Jacob wrestling with the angel. The story began with Jacob trying to hide his wives, servants, and possessions from his brother Esau. He thought Esau was coming to take revenge on him for stealing his birthright.

While Jacob was alone, in the night, at the fork of the Jabbok River, he had a wrestling match with an unidentified man. The wrestling match lasted until dawn. Though Jacob is wounded in the match, he refused to let go of his opponent until he was blessed by him. Jacob subsequently received the blessing he demanded, but the stranger dislocated the socket of Jacob's hip. Then the wrestler granted him a new name: "God-wrestler—Israel." (Genesis 32:25-28).

Based on astute exegetical reflection on the text, it is clear Jacob did not necessarily get what he sought. The blessing he received is in line with the covenantal agreement God made with Abraham. He did not get anything more than what God had already promised. To the contrary, he experienced great physical pain by trying to force God's hand in a wrestling match.

In truth, I think Jacob simply wanted God to guarantee that Esau was not going to kill him and take away his family and possessions. The blessing he desperately wanted was a result of his guilt and fear. The wrestling match, I think, was about God forcing Jacob to surrender his identity as the trickster he was, so he could become the covenantal patriarch God wanted him to become.

QUESTIONS FOR PERSONAL REFLECTION

PRAYER IS NOT FORCING GOD'S HAND

(Genesis 32:22-31)

Why is it sinful and counterproductive to pressure God when we pray?

You can't pressure God to do anything. God is self sustaining and has no weakness. We need him, He don't need us.

What happens when we try to pressure God?

You don't get what you pray for

What did Jacob learn about God in Genesis 32:22-31?

That he can't pressure God to answer prayer

No one has the Standing to make any demands on God. God moves because of His love for us.

Why do you think Jacob was wounded in the hip when he tried to force God to bless him?

His wrestling with the angel caused his wound when he could have repented and then ask in pray that God's will be done

CONCLUSION

As I was writing this chapter on what prayer is not, the Lord said to me during one of my morning-prayer walks, "You see why I haven't answered many of your prayers?" He told me that I had been praying the wrong way for years. The Almighty brought to my memory the times I used prayer to beg Him to do things that were not according to His will for my life. I also recalled the times I tried to make deals with God. And when my answer was delayed or denied, I prayed out of desperation, or tried to force God's hand to do what I needed him to do.

I am confident that I am not the only one who has been praying the wrong way. People who get frustrated with God for not answering their prayers do not have a good understanding of the exercise of prayer. They go through the motion of prayer, but they do not understand how to pray or why prayer works.

Some Christians believe all they have to do is to persevere in prayer and God will give them what they are ask for. That idea comes from a misinterpretation of Luke 18:1-8. An exegetical look at the text highlights the reasons the judge granted the woman's petition. First, the woman did not beg, or make a deal, or try to tell the judge something he did not know, or act out of desperation, or make a lengthy plea each time she went before the judge, or try to force his hand. Instead, she went to the judge with one simple request: *Grant me justice against my adversary.*

Her request was morally sensible, and just. It was practical and it was not selfish. Her approach was humble, and though she was perplexed, she was not in despair. There is a sense of honorability in her request; and her persistence speaks to that sense of honor. That is why the judge granted her request.

It is a waste of time to keep asking God for the same thing, the wrong way. Persistence in prayer without a proper understanding how to communicate with God, leads to spiritual frustration. If you are frustrated with God because He has not answered your petition, you need to go back to the drawing board and see if you are doing one of the six things mentioned in this chapter.

In the end, God delights in having a healthy and honest conversation with us. He wants us to talk to him about everything and anything. It is also good to know that sometimes the purpose of prayer is not to get anything specific. However, it is to be in the presence of God and to express our dependency on Him.

Indeed, there are times when I just want my children to talk to me without asking me for anything. Sometimes, I just want to know what is going on in their lives though I am not necessarily going to fix their problems for them. Every now and then, my oldest daughter will call me and say, "Dad, I have an issue, and I just want you to listen." I just let her talk and listen attentively. In the end, I do not try to solve anything. I let her figure it out on her own.

Some things God wants us to figure out on our own. Many people pray for good health or healing. However, they refuse to exercise and eat a healthy diet. God is not going to wave a magic wand to give us perfect health if we refuse to be good stewards of our body. Same thing can be said for those praying for financial blessings, but refuse to take responsibility for their spending habits. That is why James says in James 4:3, *When you ask, you do not receive, because you ask with wrong motives, that you may spend what you get on your pleasures.*

God is not a Genie who grants wishes. He is a supplier of needs and a regulator of minds. Everything He does is for His glory, and not to satisfy our desires. That is why it is necessary to have a broader understanding of the characteristics of prayer in order to pray more effectually.

The goal of this book is not only to teach people how to pray, it is also to help them cultivate a life of effectual prayer. By learning what prayer is not, we can begin to explore what prayer is, so our conversation with God can be more liberating, empowering and life transforming. In chapter II of this book, I explain what prayer is by highlighting the six characteristics of prayer.

SMALL GROUP DISCUSSION

The Question: Do you know what prayer is not?
The Point: When we know what prayer is, we can pray more effectually.

Background Passage: James 4:2-3
Lesson Passage: James 4:2-3
Memory Verse: James 4:3

Introduction

Many people get frustrated in their prayer life because they have a misunderstanding about prayer, its characteristics, its purpose and its power. Others stop praying altogether because they think prayer is a waste of time when, in reality, their prayer is misinformed and dysfunctional. It is imperative for Christians to understand what prayer is not so we can learn to pray more effectually.

The purpose of this chapter is to highlight the misperceptions about prayer based on what Jesus taught his disciples about prayer in Matthew 11:1-11, and based on what James said about prayer in James

4:2-3. Unless you know what prayer is not, you will not know what effectual prayer is. Thus, no matter how much time you invest in prayer, it will not work.

Background/Context

THERE ARE 21 PASSAGES IN THE NEW TESTAMENT THAT CAPTURES JESUS' teaching on prayer. He also told two parables about prayer (Luke 18:1–14). Jesus not only taught about prayer, He had a dynamic and consistent prayer life, though He did not need any material blessings from the Father. During His three years of ministry, the Bible records Jesus praying 25 different times.

Prayer was an essential aspect of Jesus' spirituality and ministry. He was intentional about teaching His disciples the fundamentals of prayer so they would be able to communicate more effectively with the Father and with Him after His ascension to heaven. The fact that the disciples asked to be taught how to pray reflect the significance of prayer for spiritual growth and maturity.

For many people in Jesus' socio-historical context, prayer was just a religious exercise practiced by those who believed in a deity. Many Jews in the Old and New Testament used prayer as a way to demonstrate their identity as the chosen people of God. Jesus criticized many Jewish religious leaders for the attitude with which they prayed. He wanted his contemporaries, subsequently us, to learn to pray more fervently and effectually.

QUESTIONS FOR SMALL GROUP DISCUSSION

What is your definition of prayer?

Communicating with God

What did Jesus teach his disciples about prayer?

He taught them to pray a certain way - Matt 6 So the were able to communicate more effectively

How many passages in the New Testament captures Jesus' teaching about prayer?

21 passages

What is unique about Christian prayer?

We allow the Holy Spirit to make intercession for us

What are the 6 deficient approaches to prayer mentioned in chapter 1 of the book "A 30-Day Guide to a Dynamic Prayer Life: Learning to Pray Like Jesus?"

1) That its unidirectional (one way
2) It's a wasteful exercise
3) distrust in prayer
4) Begging in prayer
5) Trying to Negotiate in prayer
6) Trying to bribe God

PRAYER TIPS FOR THIS CHAPTER

Pray for greater understanding about the exercise of prayer. Ask the Holy Spirit to help you become more effectual in your prayer life. Pay attention to the things you say when you pray. Try to avoid the six misconceptions about prayer discussed in Chapter I.

Life Application Questions

1. After reading this chapter, how are you going to avoid the mistakes many people make when they pray?
2. How can knowing what prayer is not help strengthen your prayer life?
3. Which one of the six misconceptions about prayer reflect your attitude about prayer?

Sample Prayer

Blessed Lord, You who discern the thoughts and can judge the heart of your people, please reveal to me the mistakes we make when I pray. May my prayers be as a sweet offering before Your throne! Take away my desire to beg or negotiate when I pray. Even in my lament, help me trust in your faithfulness and not pray out of desperation. I trust in Your providential love and find comfort in Your faithfulness.

CHAPTER II

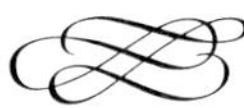

THE CHARACTERISTICS OF PRAYER

One day Jesus was praying in a certain place. When he finished, one of his disciples said to him, "Lord, teach us to pray, just as John taught his disciples." He said to them, "When you pray, say:
"'Father, hallowed be your name,
your kingdom come.
Give us each day our daily bread.
Forgive us our sins,
for we also forgive everyone who sins against us.
And lead us not into temptation,'" Luke 11:1-4

Jesus understood the necessity for His disciples to know how to pray. He knew His time on earth was coming to an end; and prayer was the only way His disciples would be able to communicate with Him after His resurrection and ascension. Therefore, Jesus took the time to teach His disciples how to pray.

I find it interesting the disciples did not know how to pray. After all, they were Jews nonetheless who were required by law to pray three times a day. Indeed, the ritual of prayer was vital to Jewish religious culture. Prayer was and is, in fact, one of the pillars of Judaism.

The disciples were not the only people who did not know how to pray. Jesus spent an inordinate amount of time teaching the masses about prayer in the Sermon on the Mount. This lets us know that one can be a Christian and not know how to pray.

There is no Scripture in the Old Testament that provides instructions on how to pray. Whereas in the Old Testament the Israelites were expected to pray three times a day (morning, afternoon, and evening), there is no clear scriptural evidence that they knew how to pray effectually. Perhaps this is because the priests were tasked with making sacrificial offerings for the people, and the prophets were responsible for interceding to God on behalf of the people.

Prayer in the Old Testament was more ritualistic. It is one of the pillars of the Jewish faith mandated by the Torah. Yet we can see many of the characteristics of an effectual prayer throughout the Old Testament.

Prayer played a vital role in the communal life of Old Testament believers. It was the primary way for the Israelites to cultivate their covenantal relationship with God. Old Testament Jews prayed to share in the life of a worshipping community.

In the earliest books of the Old Testament, prayer tended to be a spontaneous, individual, and an unorganized form of petition and/or thanksgiving. However, beginning in Deuteronomy, the structure of prayer began to be more organized, as basic liturgical guidelines were provided to the worshipping community. Prayer continued to evolve in the post-Exodus era to a more organized religious exercise that became standardized in Jewish religious practices.

David is arguably the most prolific prayer warrior in the Old Testament. Preliminary analysis of his prayer life teaches us much about the characteristics of his prayer. David was intentional in his commitment to commune with God in prayer. He was a proponent of both communal and individual prayer.

There are five key lessons we can learn from David's theology of worship.

First. David believed worship of God should be uninhibited. Prayer was David's doorway to worship God.

Second. David is very precise about who is the object of his worship and the subject of his praise. In Psalm 22:3 he said, you are the one Israel praises. In Psalm 25, David demonstrates his worship of God transcends his circumstance. Thus, even his prayer of lament is worship centered.

Third. David used prayer as a form of worship. Worship of the God of Israel was a priority for David. David worshiped God with reverence and a sense of awe. He often laid prostrate before the Lord when he prayed. David did not allow the dignity of the worship experienced to be watered-down by anyone. Nor did he allow anything or anyone to violate the sacredness of his prayer time with God.

Fourth. David often rehearsed God's promises to confirm his willingness to stand on the faithfulness of God during prayer. He did not hesitate to quote God's promises and remind the Lord what he said he would do. Nor did he question God's faithfulness or the Almighty's memory. I think these behaviors were more to let God know that he remembered God's promises and was depending on those promises to come to pass.

Fifth. David readily acknowledged his dependence upon God to rescue him from his enemies, and he willingly confessed his sins in prayer because he knew unconfessed sin would hinder his relationship with God. David prayed repeatedly for mercy, wisdom and strength because he knew he could not carry the burden of leading the people of God without the help of God. He did not try to hide anything from God, nor did David try to be ambiguous in his intent or motive in prayer.

Interestingly, David did not use prayer as a begging session. His petitions were primarily focused on deliverance from enemies. He was more concerned about spiritual cleansing and consecration than prosperity.

David used prayer as a spiritual strategy session, as well. His prayer language is transparent and straightforward. He often sought God's instruction and direction in dealing with his enemies, in making decisions for his kingdom, in developing the insights for spiritual maturity, and to acquire the necessary wisdom to lead the Jewish people.

We learn from David that prayer is a practical conversation fueled by one's faith in God. Prayer must be sincere in its expression, and should always be done in a worshipful disposition. David teaches believers that prayer must be structured. Prayer must be worshipful, confessional, and part of one's responsiveness to the prompting of the Holy Spirit; that is why David pleaded with God: *Do not cast me from your presence or take your Holy Spirit from me.* (Psalm 51:11)

There is yet another characteristic of David's prayer that should be highlighted. David uses the language of prayer to both express and strengthen his intimacy with God. He confided in God about his personal struggles. David celebrated his victories with God in prayer. In his lament, he demonstrates his limited understanding of God's divine plans. Many of David's prayers were complaints against his enemies. In some cases, he lamented God's delayed response to his adversity. His prayer life reveals his trust in God's providential love, and his steadfast commitment to serve the Almighty with all his heart and lean not unto his own understanding (Proverbs 3:5).

David was intentional about his individual prayer life. It was in his alone time with God that he confessed his sin of murder and adultery to God in Psalm 51. The imagery the Psalm reflects is that of a broken and contrite King who goes into his prayer closet for personal introspection that leads to transformation.

David bared his soul in Psalm 51, and sought spiritual healing from the Lord in ways that no one else has ever done. What we read in that psalm is a convicted sinner who bares his soul before his God without reservation. In that Psalm, we sense his fears, we hear his guilt and shame, and we can appreciate his desire for reconciliation and restoration.

Much like David, prayer was a mode of worship for Daniel. He steadfastly prayed to commune with God while living in a pagan land. There are three key aspects to Daniel's prayer life that should be highlighted. **First**, Daniel prayed according to his knowledge of the Scriptures (Daniel 9:3). His prayer life was informed by the prophetic writings of Jeremiah. **Second**, his prayers were enhanced by fasting, and based on his knowledge of the character of God. **Thirdly**, Daniel's prayers are confessional, and reflect a profound reverence for God. His prayers were not self-serving. He prayed fervently for God to forgive his fellow Israelites and turn away from His anger and wrath upon Jerusalem (Daniel 9:11).

Daniel was renowned for his prayer life. He was a man of intercession, integrity, self-control, spiritual confidence, humility, integrity. He also had tremendous influence in the Babylonian courts. In Daniel chapter 6, he was thrown into a lion's den because of his refusal to obey the king's decree that he could not pray to any other god but King Darius. Verse 10, tells us that Daniel continued to pray three times a day with his face toward Jerusalem, notwithstanding the fact he could be arrested and thrown into the lion's den.

Daniel did not allow his circumstance to dictate the fervency of his prayer life. Though he was under constant spiritual attack, he waited patiently for the Lord's will to be done. Chapter 10 says Daniel also prayed in the spirit. He communicated with God through dreams and visions. This indicates that prayer was not just a spiritual activity for Daniel or a ritual. Prayer was a habitus that shaped Daniel's relationship with God, and informed the way he lived in the Babylonian courts. Notwithstanding the influence Daniel had as a governor and chief interpreter of dreams to the king, Daniel did not turn to the King of Babylon for help. Instead, he persistently turned to the Lord God and pleaded with Him in prayer, petition, and fasting (v. 3).

Notwithstanding the legacy of prayer that abounds throughout the Old Testament, Jesus felt it necessary to teach His disciples the fundamental characteristics of prayer. Jesus's teaching on prayer highlight eight major characteristics of prayer.

DAY 7

PRAYER AS AN INDIVIDUAL SPIRITUAL EXERCISE

Prayer is both an individual and a communal spiritual exercise. In Matthew 6:5-15, Jesus cautions His followers to cultivate their individual prayer life, and have their private process to pray. After all, God wants us to relate to Him individually as well as communally. Jesus told His disciples to go into their private room and pray to the Father in secret. This stresses the intimate characteristics of prayer. The purpose of this secrecy is so that we will learn to deepen our individual relationship with our Father in Heaven.

It is in the privacy of our individual prayer we have the space for heartfelt confession. There are some things we may want to confess to God that we may not want others to hear. In the privacy of individual prayer, we can repent more earnestly and honestly without worrying about being judged. When we are alone with God, our true self comes to the forefront and we are able to fellowship with God in spirit and in truth.

In our alone time with God we can tune into the frequency of his voice more intentionally. My most satisfying spiritual experience is when I am meditating alone in a private space. Some people get bored and are unable to have focused prayer when they are alone with God. This is because we live in a world that is distracted. For most people, their minds wander when they are alone. It is as if they are afraid to acknowledge their true self.

Jesus told his disciples to go into their private room and pray to the Father in secret because He wants us to be focused in our time with God. As much as communal prayer is powerful and spiritually uplifting, it can also be distracting. It is encouraging for us to have an individual prayer life because many people cannot hear God speaking to them in prayer since they are so busy listening to the prayer of the person standing next to them.

Throughout His earthly ministry, Jesus would often withdraw to a private place to pray alone (Luke 5:16). This was not easy for the Lord because He was often followed by large crowds of individuals that wanted him to perform miracles. Yet He was intentional about carving out the space for individual prayer to sustain his intimacy with the Father.

When we pray alone, we can be more specific in our petitions, and more transparent in our confessions. Alone, we can pray without shame and guilt, and we do not have to pretend to be someone or something we are not. Solitude forces us to find our spiritual voice so we can communicate with the Lord more effectually.

Our individual prayer life should amplify and reinforce our communal prayer life. It is indeed difficult to pray communally if we do not have an individual prayer life. There is much power when two or more people come together to pray in Jesus name. When two or more people who do not have a prayer life come together to pray, that power is not as palpable. I have been in places where many people come together to pray and I felt being there was a waste of my time because these individuals were not cultivating a life of individual prayer.

Growing up, I remember my mother used to drag me to different prayer meetings every day. My mother was a prayer warrior who relished the opportunity to have intimacy with God. Because of her private prayer life, she had such a powerful communal prayer life. People would often come to my mother and ask her to pray for them because they knew she had an effectual prayer life.

QUESTIONS FOR PERSONAL REFLECTION

PRAYER AS AN INDIVIDUAL SPIRITUAL EXERCISE

(Matthew 6:5-15)

What did Jesus tell the disciples they should do when praying?

Go into their [illegible] private rooms
and pray to their father in Secret

List 3 benefits of personal prayer!

We can tune into the frequency of His Voice more intently
fellowship with God more truthfully and honestly in Spirit
We have the space for heart felt Confession

What lessons can we learn from David's prayer in Psalm 51?

David had real faith in God - We should too
It ok for you to bare you soul to God
Be intentional about my prayer life

What is the relationship between personal and communal prayer?

Our personal prayer should amplify and reinforce our communal prayer

What are the benefits of solitude for our prayer life?

Solitude forces us to find our Spiritual Voice so we can Communicate with the Lord more effectually

DAY 8

PRAYER AS A COMMUNAL SPIRITUAL EXERCISE

There might be times when a believer's faith may hinder their prayer life. In such situations, communal prayer can be very beneficial. Having others pray with us can give us spiritual support we need to overcome a faith crisis.

Communal prayer is a type of spiritual reinforcement. I am often amazed at how professional teams perform exponentially better when they are playing at home versus when they are playing away. That is undoubtedly because of the encouragement from their cheering fans.

The feeling of being encouraged by thousands of fans is vital to a professional team's successor to any athlete. The same thing can be said for communal prayer. The feeling of having two or more people joining in prayer is both inspiring and invigorating.

One benefit of communal prayer is that we pray more fervently when others join us in prayer. During my first pastorate, I used to have all night prayer services (7PM to 7AM) at the church twice per year. Amazingly, some of the people who stayed for the prayer service duration struggled to pray for five minutes on their own. Yet, when they prayed in community with other believers, they could pray for hours at a time.

Another benefit of communal prayer is that we are more invigorated to pray when we pray with others. We can quickly get discouraged or lose focus when we pray alone. A third benefit of communal pray is that it helps to embolden our faith and makes us more hopeful about a better outcome. Hearing other people intercede for us makes us more confident. It helps us to have a sense of hopeful expectation. Yet another benefit of communal prayer is that it fosters a spirit of collective worship that is not possible to cultivate through individual prayer. That does not mean a believer cannot worship God during their particular time of prayer.

In 2 Chronicles 20, we read the story of Jehoshaphat's defeat of the Moabites and Ammonites with some of the Meunites who came to wage war against him and Judah's people. Upon hearing the news about the vast army that was marching against him, Jehoshaphat brought Judah's people together to pray. As they were praying, the Spirit of the Lord came on Jahaziel, who told the king not to be discouraged or afraid of the vast army marching against Judah. Jahaziel told Jehoshaphat that the Lord will fight his enemies. Upon hearing that prophetic proclamation, Jehoshaphat, along with the people of Judah, worshipped the Lord. By the time Judah's men went to the place overlooking the desert to size up their adversary, (2 Chronicles 20:24), they saw only dead bodies lying on the ground. God had defeated their enemies before they could raise a spear in battle.

Had Jehoshaphat prayed alone, it would have been difficult for him to convince the people of Judah to remain hopeful and trust the Lord would deliver them. However, because the people were praying as a community, one of their own prophesied, and the rest became emboldened by that prophesy. Ultimately, they prevailed against their enemies, not by military might, but through the power of communal prayer.

The Church of Jesus Christ was built on the foundation of communal prayer in the upper room on the day of Pentecost (Acts 2:1-4). The New Testament church grew exponentially because the believers, *devoted themselves to the apostles' teaching and to fellowship, to the breaking of bread and to prayer* (Acts 2:42). Apostle Peter was miraculously freed from prison by an angel of the Lord because the church's saints came together to "earnestly pray to God for him" (Acts 12:5).

The main take away here is that prayer can be done individually or communally. The effectiveness of our prayer does not depend on how we pray. Instead, it is the God to whom we pray, how we approach God in prayer and the strength of our faith in God that makes prayer effectual.

QUESTIONS FOR PERSONAL REFLECTION

PRAYER AS A COMMUNAL SPIRITUAL EXERCISE

(2 Chronicles 20)

How would you define communal prayer?

It's having others pray with us which gives us Spiritual Support. It's a type of Spiritual reinforcement

What are the benefits of communal prayer?

Benefits are more fervent prayers, we more invigorated to pray, it fosters a spirit of Collective worship

What lessons can we learn about the impact of communal prayer in 2 Chronicles 20?

There is power in communal prayer and God answers by Speaking to those praying in faith and according to His word/will

What role did communal prayer played in the building of the Church?

The Church was built on the foundation of Communal prayer in the upper ROOM

Do you think your prayer is more effectual when you pray alone or when you pray with other people? Why or why not?

I think both because in either Setting my faith and trust in Him I'm in expectation of answered prayers.

DAY 9

THE IMPORTANCE OF CONFESSION IN PRAYER

The preamble to any prayer—communal or individual—must be confession, followed by repentance. Prayer, above all, is a conversation with a Perfect and Holy God. As sinful beings, we are obligated to confess our sins to find forgiveness for our unrighteousness. Thus, John reminds us *if we confess our sins, God is faithful and just to forgive us*, and He will hear our prayers.

Whereas God already knows the things we have done, we cannot repent until we have confessed. When we confess our sins, we prevent the enemy from using guilt and shame to keep us in spiritual bondage. Evil—like a deadly virus—festers in secrecy. When we expose our wickedness to the Lord, we are beginning our journey toward spiritual healing.

Before we make any petition before the Lord, we must confess our sins—known and unknown, so we can purge our spirit to make room for God's Holy Spirit to intercede on our behalf. Through confession, we express humble contrition before a Perfect God, genuine gratitude for our redemption through Christ, as well as the faith-filled appropriation of the grace of reconciliation.

Confession, then is the first step towards reconciliation. It is indeed the pathway to reconciliation. Confession is a spirit-filled expression of our genuine need for God's sanctifying grace. Through confession, we remove the veil of sin that blocks our access to God, and we position ourselves to receive mercy from the Almighty.

The second step is repentance, so there can be restoration. Sin puts enmity between God and His creation. How can we make any request, or even dare to come boldly before God's throne of grace through prayer, without repentance? To repent is to express sorrow for our sins. It is a spiritual decision not to commit the same sin again. The root word for repentance in Greek implies someone going in the wrong direction and turning to go the other way.

Not only do we have to confess our sins and repent of all unrighteousness, but we also have to demonstrate profound reverence for God in prayer. A prayer is an act of grace because of God's unfailing love through Jesus Christ. God does not need to hear our prayers. He solicits them because of His unfailing mercy to His creation. Nevertheless, we must approach God in a spirit of spiritual awe.

QUESTIONS FOR PERSONAL REFLECTION

THE IMPORTANCE OF CONFESSION IN PRAYER

(Matthew 6:9-13)

What is confession, and why should we confess our sins when we pray?

Confession is our way of expressing in prayer humble contrition before a Perfect God. It's the first step towards reconciliation.

Are the steps to reconciliation with God mentioned in Chapter 2?

yes, David Confessed his sins in prayer because he knew unconfessed sin would hinder his relationship with God.

What is the relationship between confession and repentance?

We cannot Repent until we have confessed our sins. - Repentance change of mind and direction!

How does confession enhance our prayer life?

We remove the veil of sin that blocks our access to God and we position ourselves to receive mercy from God.

What sins are you intentionally not confessing when you pray? Why not?

Sins unknown because I don't know what they are?

DAY 10

PRAYER MUST BE REVERENTIAL

In the Lord's prayer, Jesus taught the disciples to say *Our Father in heaven, hallowed be your name.* When we break down the introduction to this prayer, we can clearly see Jesus is teaching His disciples that every prayer must be characterized by a profound reverence for God. To that point, He begins the prayer with "Our Father." The title "Father" signifies God's role as the life-giver, the authority, the source of all existence, and powerful protector, often viewed as immense, omnipotent, omniscient, omnipresent with infinite power and charity that goes beyond human understanding [1]. Therefore, God is not to be defied, He cannot be denied, and He should not be disobeyed. The ancient near east understanding of a father implies respect and reverence. A father occupies the highest place of honor in the family hierarchy.

When we pray, we do not appeal to an earthly father. Rather, we pray to our Heavenly Father. The location of this Father demands our worship and adoration. God is the uncreated creator to whom we owe our reverence. That is why Jesus taught His disciples to say, "Hallow be."

The word "hallow" means sacred and revered. It denotes respect and deference. Prayer is a conversation with the *one who is able to do exceedingly and more abundantly than we can ask or imagine* (Ephesians 3:20). The one whose name is Hallowed in Heaven and on earth. Therefore, it must be characterized by a profound sense of awe and reverence for Him.

Because the God to whom we pray is our Father whose name is hallowed, we do not have to use empty phrases in our prayer. In Matthew 6:7, Jesus taught His disciples that their prayer should be specific and meaningful. These two characteristics of prayer warrant further commentary. The specificity of prayer does not have anything to do with the length of the prayer. The point that Jesus made in Matthew 6:7 is that we cannot impress God with our many words when we pray. It is not how much we say, but it is the spirit with which we say those words that makes prayer effectual. Since God already knows what we need before we ask, we can be judicious with our words in our prayer.

God is our Father. He does not need us to write a dissertation to ask Him for what we need. He invites us to ask so we can receive (Matthew 7:7). However, we have to be specific in our requests. For example, I often tell people who are unemployed, to be specific in their petition to God for employment. They should not only ask for a job, but they should ask for the type of job they desire, what company they want to work for, and the salary they want to make. If God is powerful enough to give them a job, He can also give them the desires of their heart (Psalm 37:4).

The person I mentioned in Chapter I, who prayed for over an hour during the Sunday worship service, was just heaping up empty phrases, thinking he would be heard for his many words. No one was edified, encouraged, or uplifted by his prayer. He was praying for so many different things; he ended up not praying earnestly for any one thing.

Specificity in prayer allows us to have genuine fellowship with God. It forces us to be transparent and trust that God knows us better than we know ourselves. What impresses most people with the prayer of David is his ability to get right to the point in praying to God! When David was sad, he told the Lord he was sad. He was not reluctant to confess his sin, when necessary, or to tell God he was disappointed with the Almighty for allowing his enemy to pursue him. And, I think it is because David prayed focused prayers and had such a strong relationship with God.

---

1. Lawrence Kimbrough, 2006. *Contemplating God the Father* (B&H Books: Cambridge, 2016) p. 3.

QUESTIONS FOR PERSONAL REFLECTION

PRAYER MUST BE REVERENTIAL

(Matthew 6:7)

What does it mean to reverence God?

This means to exault and lift Him up. To adore Him

How should we reverence God when we pray?

Acknowledge Him as our Heavenly Father who can do exceedingly abundantly above all we can ask or think.

What did Jesus teach his disciples about prayer in Matthew 6:7?

He taught them that their prayer should be specific and meaningful

Why should our prayer be specific?

They should be specific so we will receive exactly what we want. This allows us to have genuine fellowship with God.

How should we "hallow" the name of God in our Christian life?

We do this by appealing to Him as our Heavenly Father and respect and revere Him

DAY 11

PRAYER MUST BE SPIRITUALLY MEANINGFUL

Not only does our prayer have to be specific, they also have to be spiritually meaningful. Prayer is not so much about what we need, as much as it is about what God wants to do for us and in us. Most people do not think about the impact or consequence of receiving what they ask for in prayer. They do not think about whether what they are asking for will hinder their spiritual growth and maturity.

When I was in college, I played the lottery and prayed to God to win and become an instant millionaire. My petition to win the lottery was born out of greed and covetousness. It had no spiritual basis. My plan was to become an influential businessperson, even if winning meant forsaking my first love for Christ. Every time I went before God with my request, I was trivializing the exercise of prayer and turning it into a Christmas wish list. God could not and would not have answered such prayer because it was spiritually meaningless. That is precisely what James is talking about in James 4:3, *When you ask, you do not receive, because you ask with wrong motives, that you may spend what you get on your pleasures. Check page reference above.*

Indeed, I had somehow convinced myself that if I won the lottery, I would help friends, loved ones, and the poor, I failed to realize that

God does not need me to win the lottery to take care of the poor and needy. He has been caring for His creation since the beginning of time. He will continue to do so with or without me.

In hindsight, I should have been praying that God would use me just as I was to His glory. I did not need to become a millionaire to be of service to the kingdom of God. Indeed, I have been working in ministry since I graduated from college, even though I did not win the lottery.

What is it that makes a prayer spiritually meaningful? How do we know if we are praying meaningfully? Those are not easy questions to answer. When we are hard-pressed on every side, we instinctively want God to deliver us, open up the windows of heaven and pour out his blessing upon our lives. If our deliverance is delayed, we can become obstinate and resentful of God, especially if we see other people prospering.

The only way for a prayer to be spiritually meaningful is to prioritize God's divine purpose over our desire. It is the Holy Spirit who gives spiritual meaning to our prayers. We need the Holy Spirit to saturate our soul and give us the spiritual language to speak with God in prayer so our prayer can be meaningful. Have you ever had times when you were praying and sensed that your prayer was not making any sense?

To combat spiritually meaningless prayer, I want to make two recommendations. The first recommendation is to ask the Holy Spirit to tell you what to pray for. There have been times when I had to have a conversation with the Holy Spirit and confess that I did not know what to say in prayer. At times, my mind is so preoccupied with one thing or another that I need the Holy Spirit to renew my thoughts so I can pray in Spirit and in truth.

Any prayer that does not include the Holy Spirit is dead on arrival and spiritually meaningless. After all, prayer is a spiritual exercise done with a spiritual language only the Holy Spirit can teach. Without input from the Holy Spirit, our prayer will inevitably be flesh-driven. And how do we connect with a spiritual God with a flesh-driven approach?

God understands we do not know how to pray. He has appointed the Holy Spirit to intercede for us because He wants to make sure our prayer is meaningful. If we do not enlist the Holy Spirit's help for our prayer, we make it very difficult for God to hear us.

The second recommendation I have to combat spiritually meaningless prayer is to pray according to Scripture. The Scriptures have many useful purposes. 2 Timothy 3:16 says, *All Scripture is God-breathed and is useful for teaching, rebuking, correcting and training in righteousness.* Growing up, I watched my mother read a Psalm every time she was ready to pray. There were times when she was repeating Scriptures back to God in prayer.

God understands and appreciates the language of Scripture. There are many benefits to praying, according to Scripture: not the least of which is to use Holy Spirit inspired commentaries and instructions to relate to God.

All Scripture-based prayer is spiritually meaningful. The Scriptures teach us how to capture God's attention. They help to refine our language of worship. They also give us insight into what to expect from God and the most effective ways to solicit the favor of God.

In the 3rd Century, Origen of Alexandria introduced the view of Scripture as a sacrament. Other Church Fathers such as Saint Ambrose and Saint Augustine used the term Lectio Sacra (Sacred Reading) to highlight the sacred nature of reading Scripture. In the late 6th century, Saint Benedict and Pope Gregory I invented the tradition of Lectio Divina as an outcome of the early Church Fathers' commentary on the sacredness of reading Scripture.

Lectio Divina is a Benedictine practice of praying the Scriptures. Its four steps include: (1) reading a text, (2) meditating on that text, (3) praying in light of the book, and (4) contemplating the spiritual message within the text. I often follow the practice of Lectio Divina to deepen my prayer life.

I really like the idea of Scripture as a sacrament. A sacrament is a vital practice through which a believer confesses Jesus is God and Savior of the world. When we pray the Scriptures, we deepen our relationship with Christ and make ourselves available for a Pentecostal experience.

Scriptures have a multifaceted impact on the life of the believer. It renews the mind, edifies the soul, purifies the Spirit, transforms the heart, and justifies our worship. When we pray the Scriptures, we capture the heart of God and monopolize His attention. Praying the Scriptures is an existential cry of a soul yearning to be centered in Christ and participating in a relationship of loving union with the Triune God.

I think of prayer as a letter to God. When that letter is replete with the words the Almighty has revealed about Himself, it most certainly serenades His heart and hijacks His attention. The result is that the Holy Spirit revives our Spirit and satisfies the cravings of our soul such that we become satisfied even if our petition is not answered. Those who take the time to pray the Scriptures will discover God at a deeper level.

QUESTIONS FOR PERSONAL REFLECTION

PRAYER MUST BE SPIRITUALLY MEANINGFUL

(Ephesians 6:18)

How can we make our prayer spiritually meaningful?

We must prioritize God's devine purpose. The Holy Spirit give meaning to our prayers

How do we know if our prayer is spiritually meaningful?

If our prayer is about what God wants to do for us and in us. We must pray according to His will/word

What is the role of the Holy Spirit in helping to make our prayer spiritually meaningful?

The Holy Spirit saturates our Soul and gives us the Spiritual language to speak with God in prayer

What does it mean to pray according to Scripture?

This means to pray the word of God to God. All scripture based prayer is meaningful. I get's God's attention

What are the four steps included in the Benedictine practice of praying the Scriptures?

1) Reading A text
2) Meditating on that text
3) Praying in light of the book
4) Contemplating the spiritual message within the text.

DAY 12

PRAYER REQUIRES FAITH

Not only do prayers have to be specific and spiritually meaningful, prayer also has to be bathed in faith. In Mark 11:24, Jesus told his disciples, *Therefore I tell you, whatever you ask in prayer, believe that you receive it, and you will*. Praying without faith is a wasted exercise. *And without faith it is impossible to please God, because anyone who comes to him must believe that he exists and that he rewards those who earnestly seek him* (Hebrews 11:6).

Faith is not a concept or an emotion. It is not a feeling or an admonition. Faith in God is a choice. We have to choose to believe before we can trust that God will hear and answer our prayer. Faith in God is not explainable. It is an existential necessity and a spiritual experience that defines our humanity. I cannot convince anyone to believe in God. This is a choice a person has to make for himself or herself. However, those who make that choice as I have will discover that God rewards our faith in Him with His unfailing grace and with His unconditional love.

It is our faith that identifies us as redeemed sinners and gives us unfettered access to the throne of grace through prayer. When we pray, our identity is authenticated by our faith. Then the Holy Spirit intercedes for us because we have the badge of faith.

As members of the covenant community (Church), we have faith that God hears our every groan and will send spiritual reinforcement to sustain us in times of hardships. We also benefit from the prayer and support of other Christians who are members of the covenant community. Therefore, we do not grieve like people without hope (1 Thessalonians 4:13). We live with faith in the knowledge that *all things will work together for our good*, because of our badge of faith.

From a practical perspective, it does not make sense to request something from someone we do not think has the power and ability to honor the request. Those who pray to God without faith are disrespecting His Omnipotence. Praying with faith demonstrates confidence and trust in Almighty God Who is able to do what we need Him to do.

Faith is the grease that gets God's wheel of benevolent love to move. We have to pray with boldness because we are the children of God. As children of God, Christians can hope for blessings in this life and eternal fellowship with God in the next. We can trust that God will hear and answer our prayer according to His perfect will. The Almighty will supply all our needs according to His riches in glory, because of our faith in Him.

Faith is not only critical for prayer; it is necessary for achieving intimacy with God. People who believe in God, cultivate a relationship of loving union with Him. Because of this relationship, they have unfettered access to the Almighty, and trust that He will answer their petition in their time of need.

According to French theologian John Calvin, prayer is the "chief exercise of faith."[1] Calvin believes prayer is a barometer of faith in the believer's life. He is clear that one cannot pray apart from faith: "it is weakness or imperfection of faith that vitiates believers' prayers."

Moreover, Calvin argues believers must believe when they pray: "We testify by prayer, that we hope to obtain from God the grace which He has promised. Thus everyone who has no faith in the promises, prays dissemblingly." Calvin also writes that "unbelief pollutes and contaminates whatever is otherwise in [prayer's] nature sacred." He maintains that prayer without faith is a vain exercise of moving lips with an empty heart of unbelief.

It takes the audacity of faith to have an expectation that God will respond to our petition, or move on our behalf in response to our prayer. The audacity of faith gives hope in despair. For, *faith is the substance of things hoped for, the evidence of things not seen.* (Hebrews 11:1)

Because of the audacity of faith, we pray with fervency and persistency. Prayer is not only a spiritual mode of communication with God it is also a spiritual weapon in our warfare against our spiritual enemy. The enemy is determined to prevent us from accessing God's throne of grace to receive mercy in our times of need. Whenever we set out to pray, he tries to interfere in our spiritual connection with God.

God-based hope is not wishing for the best. It is not waiting to see what happens and hoping all turns out well. This hope is not a feeling or an emotion. It is based on the experiences we've had with God and our knowledge of the characters of God through His Holy Word. For those of us who believe, "Our hope is built on nothing less than Jesus' blood and righteousness; [we] dare not trust the sweetest frame, But wholly lean on Jesus' name." These powerful lyrics from the hymn "My Hope is Built on Nothing Less," speaks to the core of the difference between worldly hope and God-based hope. Paul reinforces that message in Romans 8:24, by asking the question, *for who hopes for what he sees*? That is where trust comes in. We trust God because we know He is faithful to His promises.

Every believer should have the audacity of faith. We should trust God to bless our finances, heal our diseases, elevate us in our career, and protect us from enemies seen and unseen. When we are faced with a life crisis, we should pray by faith for deliverance as we wait patiently for His redeeming grace to be manifested in our circumstance and His mercy to minister to our needs. So, we dare have faith that we will be the head and not the tail, not because we are better than others, but because our God is the God of mercy who can do more than we can ask or imagine.

---

1. John Calvin, *The Institutes of The Christian Religion*, Book 3, Chapter 20. Ed. John T. McNeil. Philadelphia: Westminster Press, 1960

QUESTIONS FOR SELF REFLECTION

PRAYER REQUIRES FAITH

(Hebrews 11:6)

What role does faith play in our prayer?

Faith plays a role in our true belief.

Give your interpretation of Hebrews 11:6.

If we don't have faith we can't please God because with out faith in Him how can you say you believe and trust in Him. Faith is believing what you can see with your physical eyes

Why is faith so essential to a right relationship with God?

People who believe in God cultivate a relationship of loving union with Him You have unfettered access to God and trust He will answer your petions in time of need.

What did John Calvin say about prayer?

Prayer is the chief exercise of faith
you can't pray apart from faith,
Believers must believe when they pray

What is your definition of "audacity of faith?"

Boldness of faith — Willing to be
bold in faith

DAY 13

PRAYING WITH FERVENCY

In Daniel 10:7-14, the Prince of Persia tried to interfere with Daniel's prayer for twenty-one days. It is naïve to assume that receiving God's answer to our prayer is automatic. Unfortunately, many Christians give up and stop praying when their answer is delayed. They do not remain fervent in prayer because they disregard the enemy's determination to block God's response to their prayer.

What is fervent prayer? It is a deep, focused, and passion-filled petition to God. Prayer in itself is aligning and communing with God the Creator. However, delving into a prayer with fervency amazingly changes not only the circumstance, but the supplicant as well. **Fervent prayer is the kind of prayer that rends down spiritual strongholds, and leads to spiritual revival.** Fervency in prayer requires participation from all our being. In praying fervently, our mind, body, and spirit have to be fully invested in the prayer exercise. During prayer, we have to forget about self and concentrate on God.

A soul that is passionate about God and seeks to commune with Him in the intimacy of prayer never ceases to intervene before the Almighty's throne of grace. When we set out to pray, Heaven must be made to feel the force of our petition, and the urgency for the Holy Spirit to intervene to God on our behalf. That is why we should not rush to pray. We must take the necessary time to make a deep, focused, and passion-filled petition to the Almighty every time we set out to pray.

Without fervency, prayer is just a casual conversation empty of spiritual power and appeal. Not every petition receives the same attention or consideration from our Father in heaven. As a parent, when my children come to me with a petition it is the fervency of their request that determines how quickly I respond.

I think God uses a priority list in answering our petitions. To us, our fervency in prayer confirms the importance and significance of our petition, thus prompting the Almighty God to respond more urgently. My point here is God is not going to pay the same level of attention to a millionaire who is asking God to help him make another million, as He does for the person who lost his job and is struggling to make ends meet. More than likely, the millionaire may not be fervent in their prayer because their need is not urgent and desperate. However, the unemployed individual's need is such that they are compelled to go before the Lord day-after-day in anguish, and even in tears because of desperation.

Fervency is born out of desperation. Hannah was so desperate that she went to the house of the Lord year after year to pray (1 Samuel 1:6-17). Jacob was so desperate for God to protect him and his family from the wrath of Esau that he fought with the angel all night long and would not let go until he received his blessing (see Genesis 32:22-32). The woman with the issue of blood was so desperate that she pressed her way through a large crowd so she can touch the hem of Jesus' robe (Luke 8:43-48).

Some believers wonder why God allows the righteous to suffer. I am not sure anyone can answer that question. What I do know is we become more fervent in prayer in times of trouble. Our prayer become more passionate, sincere, and heartfelt when we go through adversity. It is indeed a fact that I pray more earnestly when I face hardship than during my season of abundance.

A key aspect of a fervent prayer is that it is often coupled with fasting. Jesus prayed and fasted for 40 days and nights in the Judean desert in preparing to launch His ministry. In the gospel of Luke, we are told, *being in anguish, He prayed more earnestly, and His sweat was like drops of blood falling to the ground* (Luke 22:44). Though we do not have many accounts of Jesus fasting in the New Testament, He clearly spoke about the power of fasting (Mark 9:29).

Spiritual fasting sensitizes us to the Holy Spirit and makes our prayer life more effectual. It deepens our awareness of the presence of God, and helps us to be more open to God's response to our petitions. In fasting, we create the space to be fervent in prayer because we prioritize our spiritual hunger over our physical needs.

Spiritual fasting forces us to slow down so we can be more earnest in prayer. Many people do not like to fast because of the hunger pain associated with it. However, it is that very pain which deepens our communion with God in prayer. Fasting helps us to be more focused on our petition and increases the level of our passion as we pray.

Spiritual fasting is definitely an act of spiritual sacrifice that requires spiritual passion. In fasting, we communicate the urgency of our need in as much as we increase the potency of our petition. Fasting makes prayer more powerful because we become more intentional in our communication with God during fasting, and more open to hearing from God.

Imagine spending twelve, or twenty-four, or forty-eight hours focusing on God in prayer while denying every other need or desire. That type of fervency in prayer opens us up to a whole new level of spiritual power that is difficult to achieve without fasting. One thing for sure, it lets God know how sincere and committed we are to receive whatever we are fasting and praying for.

QUESTIONS FOR PERSONAL REFLECTION

PRAYING WITH FERVENCY

(1 Samuel 1:6-17)

What does it mean to be fervent in prayer?

It's a deep focused passion filled petition to God. It the kind of prayer that rends down strongholds spiritual and leads to spiritual revival

What lessons about prayer did you learned from Hannah's prayer life?

Hannah's prayer was one of desperation to have a child

What are the benefits of fervency of prayer before God?

Fervent prayer confirms importance and significance of our prayer.

Why do you think believers have to be fervent in prayer if God already knows what we need?

This takes your prayer to another level

How long do you think you have to keep bringing a petition before God?

DAY 14

PRAYING WITH PERSISTENCY

In the parable of the persistent widow (Luke 18:1-8), Jesus teaches us about the need to be persistent in prayer. Let us not forget our spiritual enemy is constantly trying to interfere with our prayer life, and trying to block us from receiving our blessings from God. In the book of Daniel, it took twenty-one days for Daniel to receive the answer God sent to him. Daniel was persistent in prayer throughout that time. Every day, he would go up to the roof of his house with his face towards Jerusalem to pray. It is because of his fervency that God sent Michael to help Daniel get his answer from God.

Persistency in prayer keeps the supplicant in the presence of God. The longer we stay in the presence of God, the less we have to worry about spiritual interference from the enemy. The widow in the parable of Luke 18:1-8, was determined to get vindication from the unjust judge. She kept going before the judge over, and over until she wore him down.

Those who tirelessly cry out to God in prayer will not only get the Almighty's attention, they will also demonstrate the type of determination that lets the spiritual enemy know they will not surrender this battle to him. Persistency in prayer comes from our faith in God. It is that faith that makes persistent prayer so potent and effectual.

The woman, in the above parable, was confident she could get justice from the judge. Her faith fueled her determination and forced the judge to deal with her. Persistent prayer intensifies our intimacy with God and solidifies our communion with the Almighty. Good things happens to those who are persistent in prayer because those who spend more time with God consistently will experience His overall blessings.

The thing many people do not realize is that those who earnestly seek God not only cultivate a relationship of loving union with the Lord, they will also enjoy unimaginable blessings because of their spiritual location. For in the presence of God there is the fullness of joy (Psalm 16:11 KJV). *God is a rewarder of those who diligently seek him* (Hebrews 11:6).

It is the student who persistently attends all classes, does all homework, and studies for all exams who often gets the best grades. Why? Because the more time the student spends with the teacher, the more that student learns about the subject. If there are areas where the student struggle with the subject, they position themselves to get extra help from the teacher because of access.

Persistent prayer is about unfettered access to God. It demonstrates a willingness to sit at our Master's feet so He hears our petition, and we can gain spiritual insight from His faithful love. It shows the supplicant is aware of God's unlimited and unrestricted ability to do what we need God to do.

One reason we have to be persistent in prayer is precisely because it may take time for God to transform our heart before He can give us our heart's desire. Many things we think we need are not necessarily good for us. Many of our requests are against the Will and purpose of God for us. Just asking God for the same wrong thing over, and over will not work.

I spent a long time asking God to let me win the lottery. The persistency in that prayer was misplaced. God needed to change my heart and transform my desire so I could develop a different perspective about financial blessings. Throughout the time I was praying to win the lottery, God was teaching me to live within my financial means, be content in every situation, and be grateful for what I already had.

Ultimately, my prayer was answered. Though it was not the answer I was expecting. What really happened is that every time I went before the Lord with that prayer request, He was changing my desire for the outcome I really needed. Slowly, but surely, I became less and less enthralled with having a lot of money, while at the same time becoming more passionate about spending time with God in prayer.

The Lord already knows we do not know what we should pray for (Romans 8:26). The more time we spend with God in prayer, the more opportunity we give the Holy Spirit to renew our mind so we can grow stronger in our faith and trust in God. It is because of faith and trust that doors are opened, sickness is healed, captives are set free, and mountains are moved.

In Exodus 17:8-15, the Israelites fought the Amalekites at Rephidim. Moses ordered Joshua to go fight in the valley while he went on top of the hill with Aaron and Hur to pray to the Lord for victory. In verse 11, we are told, as *long as Moses help up his hands, the Israelites were winning.* The trajectory of the battle was determined by the persistency of Moses in interceding for the Israelites.

The lifted hands of Moses inspired and empowered the warriors in the valley to know God was with them. It gave them the audacity to believe they could win the battle notwithstanding the size of their enemy. Without the hands lifted toward the heaven, the Israelites did not think God was with them, or that Moses was praying hard enough for their victory.

Aaron and Hur put a stone in place for Moses to sit on, and they held up his hands on both sides—so that his hands remained steady until sunset. Many people grow tired in their petition to God and give up before they can get the victory. At times, supplicants get worn out by the issues of life. They become discouraged and stop praying because their answer is delayed.

We all need an Aaron and Hur to hold up our spirits in prayer so we can be persistent in prayer. This is why communal prayer is so powerful. When we have other prayer warriors joining with us to encourage us to pray and to give us renewed energy motivates us to continue to cry out to God. Indeed, if it was not for Aaron and Hur,

Moses would have gotten tired and dropped his hands, and the Israelites would have been defeated by the Amalekites.

The Bible describes the spiritual life as a spiritual warfare. Our enemy is determined to wreak havoc in our lives and destroy us. One of the weapons given to believers by Jesus Christ to fight the enemy is prayer. The more persistent we are in prayer, the more the enemy will flee from us.

QUESTIONS FOR PERSONAL REFLECTION

PRAYING WITH PERSISTENCY

(Luke 18:1-8)

What does it mean to be persistent in prayer?

To pray persistently means you are before God in prayer and Continually in His presence

What lessons do you learn from the persistent widow about prayer?

She was persistent and her prayer was answered for Vindication

What are the benefits for persisting before God in prayer?

It itensifies our intimacy with God
It Solidifies our communion with Him
Consistently experience His overall Blessing

Why do you think many prayers are not answered?

Many prayers are not answered because people give in to the enemy and give up on God

What attitude should you have when coming before God in prayer?

Come in faith believing and he will answer.

CONCLUSION

There is a saying in jurisprudence that a person who has himself or herself for a lawyer is a fool. Only an attorney who is trained to speak the legal jargon of the legal system can effectively represent a person. It would be a mistake to be represented by a paralegal when facing a major legal challenge.

A good attorney will know about any legal precedent for a case. They will know how to cross-examine, and when to press the issue on behalf of their client. An attorney should know the characteristics of an effective legal representation and defend their client accordingly.

Most people pray to a higher power. Christians, however, must know about the characteristics that make their prayer to God effectual. Otherwise, we are losing the battle before we begin the fight. In this chapter, I highlighted eight characteristics of an effectual prayer. That does not mean there are only eight.

A deeper understanding of those characteristics will certainly enhance the potency of our prayer. There is more to prayer than a collection of words spoken in expectation of a spiritual experience or response. There are many spirits who are listening to our every words. Our prayers must be specifically addressed to God the Father in the name of Jesus.

Take the time to review the eight characteristics and think about what you need to do to deepen your prayer life. God wants us to pray fervently and effectually. He longs to hear our petitions, and to answer our prayer. Unfortunately, too many people do not understand the purpose of prayer. The next chapter focuses on eight purposes of prayer.

SMALL GROUP DISCUSSION

THE CHARACTERISTICS OF PRAYER

The Question: What are the characteristics of prayer?
The Point: Knowing the characteristics of prayer helps believers pray more fervently and effectually.

Background Passage: Psalm 66:18-20; 51:1-2
Lesson Passage: Luke 11:1-11
Memory Verse: Luke 11:2-4

Introduction

What does a godly prayer look like? What makes a prayer effectual? Many Christians seem to have mastered the art of prayer. My late mother was such a prayer warrior. She spent an inordinate amount of time in prayer. Other Christians would ask her to pray for them in their times of need. What was it about the characteristics of my mother's prayer that made it so effectual?

Becoming a prayer warrior is a learned skill. Everyone can pray, however, not everyone knows how to pray effectually. James reminds us that many people pray in error (James 4:2-3). Jesus scolded the Pharisees for not praying with the right attitude and disposition. The Bible teaches us the characteristics of prayer. Learning the characteristics of prayer is necessary for spiritual discipline and maturity.

Background/Context

LUKE 11:1-11, STATES THAT JESUS WAS PRAYING IN A CERTAIN PLACE WHEN the disciples came and asked him to teach them how to pray. In biblical times, it was customary for rabbis to teach their disciples how to pray. Thus, Jesus' disciples asked him to teach them the right way to pray. There is no doubt the disciples had seen and heard many other people pray in their lifetime, however, there was something unique about Jesus' prayer life.

Jesus took the time to teach the disciples the characteristics of prayer through a simple yet profound prayer. That prayer highlights five key theological understanding of what prayer is and to whom we pray. **First,** it confirms the intimate relationship between the Creator and His creation- He is our father. **Second,** it confirms the Deity of God as the Lord of the heavens. **Third,** prayer is kingdom focused. **Fourth,** it highlights our dependency on God as our supplier of all our needs and the forgiver of our sins. **Fifth**, it closes with an affirmation of the omnipotence, sovereignty and Lordship of Almighty God.

Prayer cannot be done haphazardly. Rather, it requires the one who prays to be purposeful about the "when, the how and the why of prayer." Prayer is like courtship. Through prayer, we serenade God with our love language as we express our total dependency on Him, and acknowledge the necessity of His presence in our lives.

QUESTIONS FOR SMALL GROUP DISCUSSION

What is the difference between prayer in the Old Testament and the New Testament?

____

____

____

In what Old Testament Book is the structure of prayer began to be more organized?

____

____

____

What are the characteristics of David's prayer mentioned in Chapter II of the book "A 30-Day Guide to a Dynamic Prayer Life: Learning to Pray Like Jesus?"

____

____

____

What are the three aspects to Daniel's prayer mentioned in Chapter II?

____

____

____

How many characteristics of prayer is mentioned by Jesus? And what are they?

____

____

____

PRAYER TIPS FOR THIS CHAPTER

Pray for the Holy Spirit to counsel you about the type of prayer appropriate for each occasion. Ask the Lord to make you more fluent in the language of prayer so you can become a Spirit-led prayer warrior. Remember, effectual prayer is not about how long one prays; it is about having the right attitude and language of prayer.

Life Application Questions

1. List 3 things you learned from this chapter about the characteristics of prayer.
2. How are you going to use the knowledge about the Characteristics of prayer to deepen your prayer life and to help others develop a stronger prayer life?
3. How would you characterize your prayer life in light of this chapter?

Sample Prayer

Blessed Lord, please teach me how to pray the way Jesus taught his disciples to pray. May my prayers be acceptable to you and reflect my gratitude for the privilege I have to have spiritual intimacy with you in prayer. Saturate my mind and heart with your Holy Spirit so I can pray more effectively and fervently. May the words of my mouth and the meditation of my heart be acceptable in your sight, Lord, my Rock and my Redeemer (Psalm 19:14; NIV).

CHAPTER III

THE PURPOSE OF PRAYER

Do not be anxious about anything, but in everything, by prayer and petition, with thanksgiving, present your requests to God. And the peace of God, which transcends all understanding, will guard your hearts and your minds in Christ Jesus. Philippians 4:6-7

When I was about ten years old, I had a dream where a giant of a person told me that God was angry with me because I was not praying. This giant pulled out a big stick and started to beat me for failing to pray. He then reminded me that I was alive because of prayer, and if I ever stopped praying, I would die. Since that time, I have been passionate about prayer and continue to make prayer a vital part of my life and spirituality.

That dream is still as vivid in my mind as it was over four decades ago. When I look back at that experience, I am convinced, God wants us to pray. The Almighty takes the initiative to invite His followers to pray for reasons we do not always understand or appreciate.

Why do people pray? Ironically, there are people with no faith in God who pray in their time of crisis. Most people pray because they want something from God. They assume prayer is something they initiate to express a need, make a petition, or an intercession. However,

I am convinced prayer is not something we initiate. Prayer is a spiritual invitation from God to commune with Him.

It is the Spirit of God who prompts our hearts to pray. It is just as physical hunger forces a person to feed his or her physical body. Our spiritual hunger also compels our soul to seek spiritual nourishment from the Almighty.

Prayer is a spiritual feeding tube through which we receive spiritual nourishment for the soul. The fundamental purpose of prayer is not to change our circumstances, or the circumstances of those for whom we intercede. The fundamental purpose of prayer is to sensitize us to the presence of God, and to draw us near the Almighty so we can be transformed into the image of Christ.

What happens when God does not change our circumstances? Should we not continue to pray? Unfortunately, many people stop praying when their circumstance does not change. I had a conversation with a self-proclaimed atheist who confessed the reason he stopped believing there is a God because he prayed when his mother was terminally ill, and God did not heal his mother. From that moment forward, he made up his mind that prayer was a waste of time, and faith in God was a fantasy.

This chapter highlights five purposes of prayer. I think it is vital to develop a healthy understanding about the purpose of prayer so we can pray more effectually, and not lose our faith when our circumstance does not change. Christians have to know that God is more concerned about the condition of our souls than our earthly comfort.

DAY 15

THE PURPOSE OF PRAYER IS TO STAY CONNECTED TO GOD

God stimulates us to pray because He wants us to remain connected to our One true power source so we can have the needed strength to fight against powers and principalities of this world. As believers, when we pray, we remind our spiritual enemy that we belong to God, and that we know from whom all of our blessings flow. Prayer is both validation of our faith and confirmation of our identity as disciples of Jesus Christ.

Our connection to God is vital to our spiritual growth, and our ability to resist the temptations of the enemy. Newborn babies have to eat regularly. In some cases, every two hours. Their mother's milk is not only good for nourishment, but it contains antibodies they need to fight diseases. Their connection with their mother is vital to their growth and development. Without that connection, a newborn may even die or experience separation anxiety.

In the same way, our soul craves for intimacy with God. Through prayer, we are able to remain connected spiritually to the One who made us more than conquerors through Jesus Christ our Lord. That connection is tantamount to spiritual lubrication for our spiritual engine.

Staying connected with God is a lifestyle of total surrender to His will. It is a willingness to die to our carnal desires and *to be hidden with Christ in God* (Colossians 3:3). This connection allows us to tune into the frequency of God's voice so we can hear His instructions for our life and ministry.

In John 15:5-7, Jesus told His disciples, *I am the vine; you are the branches. If you remain in Me and I in you, you will bear much fruit; apart from Me you can do nothing. If you do not remain in Me, you are like a branch that is thrown away and withers; such branches are picked up, thrown into the fire and burned. If you remain in Me and my words remain in you, ask whatever you wish, and it will be done for you.*

Every time I work from home, I have to log into the Virtual Private Network (VPN) for my company to access their database and work accordingly. If I do not log into the VPN, I cannot access my work emails and the central database that I use to process the clinical data I have to prepare for FDA analysis. Through VPN, I can stay in touch with my direct reports from many countries. The company spends millions to ensure their network is protected against malware and harmful viruses. I can only access the private network through a company assigned computer.

Prayer is the assigned computer God gave us to access His Heavenly private network (HPN). Jesus is the password that gives us access to this network. Without Jesus, we will wither and be thrown into the fire of hell to be burned. Every day we wake up, we have to access God's Heavenly Private Network (HPN) in the name of Jesus, so we can do God's kingdom work through prayer.

Followers of other religions are trying to access God's Heavenly Private Network without prayer in Jesus' name and without the right password. The only way to connect with God is through Christ-centered prayer. Those who do otherwise are to be denied access to God's throne of grace.

As sinful beings, you and I mess up and even backslide, every now and then. We can easily forget who we are and whose we are. The good news is that we can always call Heaven's hotline to get reconnected to the Father through prayer. When we do call (pray), we have to use our Heavenly identity as followers of Jesus.

Perhaps you have lost your password to stay connected to God's network. Consequently, you stopped praying, do not go to church, are too busy to serve, or too angry to forgive. All you have to do is call heaven's hotline through prayer and let it be known that you want to get reconnected with God in the name of Jesus. You will not be denied because of the blood of the resurrected Jesus.

QUESTIONS FOR SELF REFLECTION

THE PURPOSE OF PRAYER IS TO STAY CONNECTED TO GOD

(John 15:5-7)

Why does the Holy Spirit prompt us to pray?

He wants us to stay connected to our true power source

Why is it important to stay connected to God through prayer?

To avoid being overtaken by the things of this world

How can we access God's Heavenly Private Network (HPN)?

Through Prayer in the name of Jesus

Why do we have to pray in the name of Jesus?

No man can get to the Father except he go thru Jesus His son

What mistakes are followers of other religions making with regard to prayer?

?

DAY 16

THE PURPOSE OF PRAYER IS TO UNBURDEN OUR SOULS

David is not the only person in the Bible who used prayer to unburden his soul (Psalm 51). In 1 Kings 19:4, the great prophet Elijah was so overwhelmed with fear as he battled depression, he prayed that he might die. Elijah was troubled for the ungodliness of the Israelites. He was also burdened by his fear of Jezebel.

After traveling a day's journey into the wilderness, Elijah was physically tired and emotionally distraught. In desperation, he cried out to God. The Lord heard his prayer and sent an angel to take care of him. After some much needed rest and food, Elijah was able to travel to Mount Horeb for an encounter with God.

Prayer is spiritual therapy for many people. In some cases, it can even be used as emotional therapy. Indeed, there is something therapeutic about talking to God in prayer in our moments of distress. That is because *the Lord is close to the brokenhearted and saves those who are crushed in spirt* (Psalm 34:18).

I personally experienced God's comfort when my mother died. I spent many hours crying out to God in prayer. The Lord heard my despairing cries and comforted me from my sorrows. My grieving process would have been far more difficult if I could not been connected with God in prayer.

God in his infinite wisdom gave us prayer so we can unburden our souls from the cares of this world. In Matthew 11:28, Jesus invites us to *come to me, all you who are weary and burdened, and I will give you rest.* Prayer is the primary way people come to God when they are burdened and weary.

Prayer is not only a communication tool; it is also a survival mechanism given to us by God so we can overcome the vicissitudes of life. We get the Lord's attention when we cry out to Him in despair. For, the Lord is attentive to the cry of His children. Therefore, we should not hesitate to come to Him in times of trouble.

God offers total confidentiality. He does not condemn us for bringing our burdens to Him. Nor does He look down on those who come to Him in their hour of need. To the contrary, a little talk with God always make things better. We get a better perspective about our circumstance during and after prayer. Prayer can revitalize our spirit and give us renewed spiritual energy for our Christian journey.

Because of the original sin of Adam and Eve, human beings suffer from post-traumatic sin disorder (PTSD). The symptoms of that disorder are guilt, shame, depression, anxiety, fear, low self-esteem, pride, greed, and arrogance. Notwithstanding our achievements, or level of education, or social status, we all experience existential burnout. That is why so many people either attempt or commit suicide daily.

A large number of people are struggling with addiction to illicit drugs, alcohol, or pornography because they are looking for an escape from their spiritual PTSD. There is no medical cure or treatment for this form of PTSD. God is the only therapist who can help us deal with this condition. And the only way we can communicate with our Heavenly therapist is through prayer.

God invites us to confess our sins, because *He is faithful and just to forgive us our sins and to cleanse us from all unrighteousness* (1 John 1:9). A prayer of forgiveness can go a long way toward emotional healing. Those who know their sins have been forgiven have a different perspective about their existence. They are not burdened by a constant state of shame and guilt. Instead, they are able to live in the peace of God.

Without forgiveness, there cannot be reconciliation with the Triune God. Forgiveness is tantamount to the washing of dirty clothes. Through forgiveness, we become usable in the service of God. Not only is the stain of shame and guilt on our soul removed through forgiveness, we become renewed and restored as instruments of godliness, and proclaimers of the gospel of truth.

The burden of sin is too much for any human being to carry. The lyrics of the Christian Hymn "I Must Tell Jesus," echoes the anthem of believers who want to be free of their existential burdens:

I must tell Jesus all of my trials
I cannot bear these burdens alone
In my distress
He kindly will help me
He ever cares and loves His own

I must tell Jesus all of my troubles
He's a kind and compassionate friend
If I but ask Him
He will deliver
Make of my troubles
Quickly an end

Prayer is the only way we can tell Jesus all of our trials and troubles. Indeed, one of the primary functions of prayer is to communicate with our redeemer in times of crisis. The Lord's spiritual hotline is always open. All we have to do is cry out to God and we will get the spiritual therapy we need to rejoice in the bountiful grace of God.

QUESTIONS FOR SELF REFLECTION

THE PURPOSE OF PRAYER IS TO UNBURDEN OUR SOULS

(Psalm 51; 1 Kings 19)

How did David use prayer to unburden his soul?

David used prayer to lament and confess his sins

How did God answer Elijah's prayer of desperation?

He sent an Angel to take care of him with rest and food, then he was able to have an encounter with God

What is your understanding of prayer as a form of therapy?

It is therapeutic in that prayer can calm you and give you peace when needed

How does prayer help us cope with and survive the vicissitudes of life?

Prayer gives us peace in the mist of turmoil

What are some of the side effects of the sin of Adam and Eve?

Spiritual Separation from God
loss of the Garden of Eden due to Sin – guilt, Shame, fear

DAY 17

THE PURPOSE OF PRAYER IS TO MAKE OUR REQUESTS KNOWN TO GOD

In Philippians 4:6, we are told, *Do not be anxious about anything, but in every situation, by prayer and petition, with thanksgiving, present your requests to God*. Our Heavenly Father expects us to communicate our needs to him in prayer. We were not created to be autonomous. God is the provider of everything we need.

Our dependency on God is essential for our physical and spiritual well-being. From the moment we enter this world, we were made to deal with the ebbs and flows of life. As Job said in 14:1, *Human born of a woman is but of few days, and full of trouble*. We are troubled by the things that happen to us as individuals, and to others. The only way to cope with those troubles is to give them over to our Father in Heaven, who can deliver us from them all.

Therefore, we have to make our request known to God so we can find mercy in our times of needs. The request may be a petition for a personal need, or an intercession for someone else. Whereas, God may not grant every request, He will change us, and the people for whom we intercede: *And the peace of God, which transcends all understanding, will guard our hearts and our minds in Christ Jesus* (Philippians 4:7).

Making our request known to God in prayer should be our first and foremost response to the problems we face. This is our way of fighting back against enemies seen and unseen. It is our rallying cry, if you will, whether we have or lack the resources and the fortitude to overcome our hardships.

God offers many guarantees to those who diligently seek him in their hour of need. In Psalm 50:15, the Lord says *"and call on me in the day of trouble; I will deliver you, and you will honor me."* He invites us to present any and all, request before Him. We should never be ashamed to express our need to our Father in heaven no matter the nature of those needs.

It is human to think that when we make a request to God, He should grant the request as we have presented it. However, what if the request leads to self-destruction? What if the request is against the will of God and His plan for your life? God is not obligated to grant the request that will lead us astray. Whereas He has the power to change any situation, He is more concerned about our spiritual growth and maturity. Therefore, prayer is never a waste of time, and it should be offered at any time, for anything.

Though the Bible teaches *all things work together for the good to those who love the Lord and are called according to his purpose* (Romans 8:28), this does not mean that God will change every situation to our liking. Nevertheless, we should not hesitate to make our requests known to God. Doing so is never an exercise in futility. Rather, it is an expression of faith.

Any conversation with God is in itself rewarding. For, in the presence of God there is the fullness of joy. And, just a little talk with Jesus will make everything all right. Even when our request is not fully met, God promises us His peace in trouble. Thus, our ability to endure hardships and to persevere through our trials is strengthened.

Philippians 4:6, teaches us to reject worry and to be thankful to God for granting us access to His throne of grace through prayer so we can find mercy in our times of need. In response, we should offer thanksgiving to the one who *is able to supply all our needs according to His riches in glory* (Philippians 4:19). Then, we will be at peace even when trouble like sea billows roll into our lives.

In as much as we should always pray to God in the name of Jesus Christ, we should also exclaim that God's will be done. This is a simple, yet powerful theological phrase reminding us that making our request known to God frees us of the burdens that can vex our spirit, and ensnare us into a life of worry. As we accept Jesus' invitation according to Matthew 11:28-30, we find relief and the joy of the Lord in our soul restored.

QUESTIONS FOR SELF REFLECTION

THE PURPOSE OF PRAYER IS TO MAKE OUR REQUESTS KNOWN TO GOD

(Philippians 4:6-7)

How should we make our request known to God in prayer?

This should be done by prayer and petition, with thanksgiving

What guarantees does God provide to those who diligently seek after him?

Call on Him in the day of trouble He will deliver you and you will honor him.

What three things are we supposed to do when we pray according to Philippians 4:6?

We are Not to be anxious about anything in every situation by prayer & petition with thanksgiving present my request to God.

What type of relief do we find when we pray?

The joy of the Lord in our soul is restored

What should we do when feeling overwhelmed and perplexed by the issues of life?

Pray

DAY 18

THE PURPOSE OF PRAYER IS TO WORSHIP GOD

Warren Wiersbe describes worship as "the submission of all our nature to God. It is the quickening of conscience by His holiness; the nourishment of mind with His truth; the purifying of imagination by His beauty; the opening of the heart to His love; the surrender of will to His purpose -- and all of this gathered up in adoration, the most selfless emotion of which our nature is capable and therefore the chief remedy for that self-centeredness which is our original sin and the source of all actual sin." For Pastor and Theologian A. W. Tozer, worship "is to feel in your heart and express in some appropriate manner a humbling but delightful sense of admiring awe and astonished wonder and overpowering love in the presence of that most ancient Mystery, that Majesty which philosophers call the First Cause, but which we call Our Father Which Art in Heaven."

Worship means different things to different people. For me, worship is the universal language of all believers. It is a profound spiritual act of yielding to the sovereignty of God as we are enraptured by the awesomeness of His glory. This is precisely what we experience when we respond to God's invitation to commune with Him in prayer.

Through prayer, we are able to enter into the Holy of holies to worship the Lord. Worship is a natural response for any being who comes before God. Isaiah 6:1-13 gives powerful imagery of Heavenly beings worshipping God. We cannot therefore, come before God in prayer without an offering of praise and a spirit of worship. Indeed, there is an expectation of worship for any being who seeks to commune with God.

No matter our circumstance or the urgency of our need, we should always worship God before and during prayer. This is why it is a good practice to read a Psalm of worship before prayer. When we accept God's invitation to pray, we also agree to worship His majesty. Let us keep in mind God already knows what we are going to say in prayer. Therefore, the invitation to prayer is not necessarily to repeat words God already knows. Rather, it is an opportunity for Holy Communion with the Divine that requires worship.

In the 1970's, the "Centering Prayer" movement was launched by the Trappist monks of St Joseph's Abbey in Spencer, Massachusetts. This controversial spiritual practice is a method of meditation that places a strong emphasis on interior silence. The ultimate goal is to have an inward experience with God and to hear from the Divine by clearing one's mind of outside concerns so God's voice may be more discernibly heard.

Though I do not engage in that type of spiritual practice, I admit people are more apt to focus on worship during meditation prayer than at any other time of prayer. The idea of remaining silent as the mind focuses on experiencing the fullness of the Divine in order to hear a response from the Almighty compels the soul to worship in ways it does not always do when prayer is verbalized. Meditation prayer quickens our entry into the Holy of holies so we can worship God in Spirit and in Truth.

There are times when the soul is so overwhelmed with grief that prayer of lament may overshadow our desire and need to worship God during prayer. Indeed, grief and worry can diminish our need or desire to worship. We must always be careful and intentional so that our desire to offer petition and intercession does not put out the fire of our worship.

Worship comes from a heart that has been sanctified by the Holy

Spirit. In Psalm 86:12, the Psalmist says, *I will give thanks to You, O Lord my God, with all my heart, and I will glorify your name forever*. Only by the transforming power of the Holy Spirit can the heart worship God. In Ezekiel 36:26; the Lord says, *And I will give you a new heart, and a new spirit I will put within you. And I will remove the heart of stone from your flesh and give you a heart of flesh.* In Psalm 5:10, 12, David says, *Create in me a pure heart, O God, and renew a steadfast spirit within me… Grant me a willing spirit, to sustain me… The sacrifices of God are a broken spirit; a broken and contrite heart, O God, you will not despise.*

The heart of worship is a regenerated heart that is filled with reverence for God and seeks to glorify the majesty of God continuously. It is a heart that truly loves God and seeks to bring every thought to subjection unto the will of God. Such a heart seeks to ascend to the secret place of God's indwelling Holiness to make of itself an altar whereon it may offer to God the sacrifice of pure love, praise and pure reverence (St John of the Cross).

It takes more than singing songs and verbalizing words of acclamation unto God to develop a heart of worship. A heart of worship is a state of being. It is not an act to perform. It is a state of consciousness wherein the worshipper is in a constant state of awareness of the awesomeness of God and surrenders all desires and all strange affections for the sake of pure communion with God.

This type of worship does not necessarily need to be verbalized, it must be realized. It does not need to be publicized, for it is too precious to be trivialized. Jesus nurtured a heart of worship as He was in constant fellowship with the Father through prayer. True worship of God comes from the heart of those who trust the Almighty with all their heart and do not lean unto their own understanding (Proverbs 3:5).

QUESTIONS FOR SELF REFLECTION

THE PURPOSE OF PRAYER IS TO WORSHIP GOD

(Isaiah 6:1-13)

What is your definition of worship?

____

____

____

How is prayer a form of worship?

____

____

____

What is your preferred mode of worship?

____

____

____

Where does worship originate?

____

____

____

What is the heart of worship?

____

____

____

DAY 19

THE PURPOSE OF PRAYER IS TO CULTIVATE A RELATIONSHIP OF LOVING UNION WITH GOD

It takes time to cultivate any type of healthy relationship, particularly one with the Sovereign God who is Holy in all His ways. Unexplainably, God desires a relationship with us despite our sinfulness. Our relationship with God started in the Garden of Eden wherein Adam and Eve had unfettered access to the Almighty. Unfortunately, our access was revoked after the sin of Adam and Eve, but our relationship with God did not end.

Since the fall of Adam and Eve, God has been intentional about restoring humanity to a right relationship with Him. The incarnation of Jesus was the ultimate evidence of God's restorative plan. When Jesus arose from the grave and ascended into Heaven, the restoration project was completed. However, because we wrestle against powers and principalities, we need to be intentional about staying connected with our Father in Heaven by cultivating a relationship of loving union with Him.

There are four salient characteristics of a loving relationship with God. The first, it requires effective communication. That is why knowing the ABC's of prayer is so important. We need to learn how to communicate with the Lord effectively. It is not possible to have a right relationship with God without communicating with Him in prayer.

Prayer is two-way communication. The supplicant is not the only one who talks. God also talks to us in prayer. God uses different means to communicate with us. He uses the Bible, devotionals, sermons, people we trust and respect. God can even use nature to speak to us. He can speak to us in dreams, and use the hardships of life to communicate difficult lessons.

The challenge for most people is their spiritual ears are often clogged by the cares of this world. At times, some believers are so enamored with the world that they allow themselves to be distracted by the cacophony of voices that are striving to occupy their attention. Thus, they are unable to hear the voice they really need to hear—God.

Through prayer we are able to center our spirit and focus our soul so we can communicate with the God of our salvation. That communication informs our spirituality and strengthens our worship. It gives us access to the secret place of the Most High God so our soul can abide under the shadow of the Almighty (Psalm 91:1).

The second characteristic allows us to get to know God and become more fluent in the language He understands best. God is faithful in all His ways. He expects us to approach Him by faith, as we trust in His unfailing love. Hebrews 11:6 reminds us that *without faith it is impossible to please God.* Those words are echoed by Jesus in Mark 11:24.

The point is that a relationship of loving union with God requires trust with faith as its foundation. Prayer allows us to expand our faith. The more we pray, the stronger our faith becomes.

Those who pray persistently do so because they trust God to hear and answer their prayers. It is their faith that makes their prayers effectual. Time invested in prayer always yields a return of spiritual maturity. However, the currency for that investment is faith.

Where the seed of faith has been sown, trust and confidence in the faithfulness of God becomes automatic. The only way we can trust in the Lord with all our heart and lean not on our own understanding, is to have faith in Him. Faith allows us to submit to Him in all our ways notwithstanding our circumstance.

Besides, God is a Spirit we cannot see. How can we have a relationship of loving union with a Spirit unless we believe He is everything He says He is. When we get on our knees to pray, we are making a statement of faith. Prayer is the romance language of God. If we really want to have an intimate relationship with the divine, we have to pray earnestly and persistently by faith.

The third characteristic is a healthy and dynamic relationship requiring familiarity. We have to take the time to get to know God through His Word. Believers should not babble like pagans during prayer, nor rush the prayer process either. There is so much about God we do not know, and so much that God wants to reveal to us about His plans for our lives. Prayer should be an adventure.

We should use prayer to become more familiar with God. In our prayer, it is okay to ask God about the best way to please Him. We should ask Him to reveal to us areas of sin in our lives, and how we can best do His will. Take the necessary time to hear from the Holy Spirit and to meditate on what we hear about God from different reliable sources.

David was so familiar with God that the Lord called him a man according to His own heart. David's prayers to God were at times conversational and at other times formal. He did not waste words in prayer. However, he took his time to speak to God as a friend, sometimes as a father, at times as a deliverer, but always as his Sovereign Lord.

When people tell me they do not know what to say in prayer, I always encourage them to just start with what I call "get acquainted prayer." That is a type of prayer where the supplicant is not fluent in the language of prayer, but introduces himself or herself to the Lord in order to establish a relationship. After a couple of weeks of saying "get acquainted prayers," the supplicant becomes more familiar with God and his or her vocabulary continues to expand.

In Jeremiah 29:13, The Almighty says, *You will seek me and find me when you seek me with all your heart.* The truth is people do not pray because they do not have faith. They do not have faith because they are not familiar with God. They are not familiar with Him because they do not seek Him with all their heart. One of the most effective and rewarding ways to seek God is through prayer.

The fourth characteristic is that we cannot have a relationship of loving union with God without an investment of time. Many marriages are failing because one partner is not investing enough time to keep the passion in the marriage burning. It takes time to become familiar with God.

Sometimes we have to invest the time to wait on the Lord. The Bible assures us *But those who hope in the LORD will renew their strength. They will soar on wings like eagles; they will run and not grow weary, they will walk and not be faint* (Isaiah 40:31). At times, we have to wait on God to answer our prayer. Abraham waited for 25 years to get the son he prayed for.

The first thing Jesus did before He began His ministry was to go in the wilderness to pray for 40 days and nights. Jesus invested this time in prayer because he understood the significance of his mission for the salvation of humanity. With so much at stake, Jesus invested the time in prayer so He could be ready to face His enemies and proclaim the gift of salvation to all who believe in Him.

Too many Christians want to grow in spiritual maturity but they are not willing to invest the time to practice the spiritual disciplines of prayer, fasting, and meditation on the Word of God. When Elijah was so depressed he wanted God to kill him. The Lord made him travel 40 days to Mount Horeb so He could have a conversation with him. After that conversation Elijah's strength was renewed.

When we engage in family devotion at night, my son is always in a rush to finish his prayer. I do not rebuke him because he is still a teenager and a babe in the faith. On the other hand, invest time to pray throughout my day. And when I don't pray without ceasing, I feel an emptiness in my soul that only a conversation with God can fill.

QUESTIONS FOR SELF REFLECTION

THE PURPOSE OF PRAYER IS TO CULTIVATE A RELATIONSHIP OF LOVING UNION WITH GOD

(Psalm 91; Mark 11:24)

What are the four salient characteristics of a relationship with God?

____

____

____

What is a 'get acquainted prayer'?

____

____

____

How does prayer help us to center our spirits so we can communicate with God?

____

____

____

How would you describe your relationship with God?

____

____

____

How does prayer help us to become more familiar with God?

____

____

____

CONCLUSION

Prayer is a complex spiritual exercise with many purposes. While I highlighted some of the purposes for prayer, the purposefulness of prayer will vary depending on the individual's spiritual perspective. The important thing is for believers to realize and appreciate that prayer is a power spiritual tool they cannot do without.

Prayer is like a cell phone. When the hand held mobile phone was developed by Motorola in 1973, no one could have envisioned we would be able to do so much with that device. Today, people use cell phones to conduct multibillion dollars businesses. Some people watch movies on their cell phones. Others use it to send money to family members. The cell phone can be used to provide traveling directions, as well as for social networking purposes.

The general idea behind a cell phone is that it keeps people connected. In this same way, prayer keeps us connected with God and with the family of faith. Prayer strengthen believers for the work of ministry. Prayer is universally adaptable. Whatever the need or circumstance, we can bring it to the Lord in prayer. Since God is the one who initiates prayer and invites us to pray, it is certainly a worthwhile spiritual exercise with many benefits. It behooves believers to use it persistently so we can maximize its usefulness.

SMALL GROUP DISCUSSION

THE PURPOSE OF PRAYER

The Question: What is the purpose of prayer?
The Point: Prayer is a spiritual invitation from God to commune with Him.

Background Passage: Philippians 4:4-7; Psalm 145:18-19
Lesson Passage: Philippians 4:4-7
Memory Verse: Philippians 4:6

Introduction

God initiates the prayer conversation, not us. All we do is respond to the invitation from the Almighty by entering into dialogue with Him through prayer. Without the prompting of the Holy Spirit to pray, most people would have no desire to pray. God invites us to pray because He knows we need to stay connected to Him. Without an ongoing conversation with God, we would not know how to face the vicissitudes of life and triumph over our spiritual enemy.

Prayer has a variety of purposes for the believer. Through prayer, we are able to worship God and fellowship with Him and others in the body of Christ. Prayer helps to enhance our spiritual growth and development. We become more Christ centered through prayer. Indeed, there is more to prayer than just asking for material stuff, healing, or deliverance. Prayer is an important weapon in the arsenal of the believer. Too many Christians are not fervent in their prayer life, thus making them more spiritually vulnerable than they should be. The more we know about the purpose of prayer, the more persistent we become in our prayer life.

Background/Context

THERE ARE MANY REASONS WHY PAUL TOLD THE PHILIPPIANS NOT TO BE *anxious about anything, but by prayer and petition, with thanksgiving, to present their requests to God* (Philippians 4:6). Paul understood that prayer is an affirmation of our faith in the God who can supply all our needs. He understood that one of the best ways for Christians to remain steadfast in their Christian journey is through prayer.

Paul was so convinced of the efficacy of prayer that he commanded the Philippians to substitute anxiety with prayer. The Philippian church faced many challenges. The believers were persecuted for their faith in addition and struggled with existential crises. Prayer proved to be an effective coping mechanism that enabled the saints in Philippi to endure for the sake of Christ.

Paul urged the Philippians to take everything to God in prayer so they could continue to be encouraged and to walk in the will of God. Prayer would allow them to remain in communication with God so that *His peace that transcends all understanding would guard their hearts and minds in Christ Jesus* (v. 7). Paul was confident prayer would allow them to remain in the power of God, which alone would fan the flame of their faith through their hardships.

QUESTIONS FOR SMALL GROUP DISCUSSION

Why do you pray?

___

___

___

What is the purpose of prayer?

___

___

___

How should we respond when the Holy Spirit prompts us to pray?

___

___

___

How do you know when the Holy Spirit is prompting you to pray?

___

___

___

What are the five purposes of prayer highlighted in Chapter III of the book "A 30-Day Guide to a Dynamic Prayer Life: Learning to Pray Like Jesus?"

___

___

___

PRAYER TIPS FOR THIS CHAPTER

Pray that the Holy Spirit will help you stay connected to God through prayer. Use the time of prayer as an opportunity to unburden your soul to your Father in Heaven. Do not hesitate to let your requests be made known to Him. Savor the opportunity to worship God as you pray.

Life Application Questions

1. How do you use prayer to stay connected to God?
2. What burden have you been carrying that you can take to the Lord in prayer?
3. How can prayer help enhance your worship?
4. How often do you worship God while praying?

Sample Prayer

Holy Father, thank You for endowing me with the language of prayer so I can communicate with You in times of need. Thank you for inclining your ears to my petitions. I pray that the supplication of my heart reaches your Heavenly throne and is acceptable to you as a sacrificial offering. Please help me to be predisposed to commune with You in prayer so I can satisfy our innate desire to be in a relationship of loving union with You.

CHAPTER IV

THE POWER OF PRAYER

Is anyone among you in trouble? Let them pray. Is anyone happy? Let them sing songs of praise. Is anyone among you sick? Let them call the elders of the church to pray over them and anoint them with oil in the name of the Lord. And the prayer offered in faith will make the sick person well; the Lord will raise them up. If they have sinned, they will be forgiven. Therefore, confess your sins to each other and pray for each other so that you may be healed. The prayer of a righteous person is powerful and effective. James 5:16

If prayer is a conversation with God and a spiritual exercise, what makes it powerful? What do we mean when we talk about the power of prayer? This chapter examines the power of prayer.

The Bible is filled with accounts of miraculous things taking place because of prayer. For example, Moses prayed and the Lord opened up the Red Sea to give safe passage to the Israelites out of Egypt (Exodus 14:15). In Acts 9:40, Peter raised Tabitha from the dead through the power of prayer. And the Church of Jesus Christ was founded on the Day of Pentecost when the disciples were all together praying (Acts 2:1).

Is there any evidence in your life to substantiate the claim that prayer is a powerful spiritual tool? Have you ever prayed about something and it came-to-pass? How has the power of prayer impacted your life and your spiritual journey?

When I was a young boy, my mother used to tell the story about how prayer saved my life. According to the story, I became very sick a few weeks after birth. The doctor had given up on me and told my mother to prepare my funeral. My mother was not a born again Christian during that time. However, she went to a pastor and asked him to pray for me. That man of God prayed for me for seven days, and on the seventh day, I regained consciousness and finally ate some food. From that day forward, my mother consecrated herself, and me, to the Service of the Lord and made a vow to God that I would be His forever.

Growing up in a praying family, I witnessed firsthand the power of prayer. My mother would wake us up in the middle of the night to pray whenever she was prompted by the Holy Spirit. When my parents were short on money, God always provided food and clothing for my siblings and me because my mother prayed.

Many people in my neighborhood came to my mother for prayer. Many families were blessed, individuals healed from diseases, and lost souls came back to God because my mother prayed. I know about the power of prayer.

I want believers to be confident about the power of their prayers. If believers understood the potency of prayer, they would probably pray more earnestly and consistently. Having a timid prayer life is like going to war with a loaded machine gun but never pulling the trigger when the enemy advanced against you.

Prayer is indeed a loaded spiritual firearm. However, like any other firearm it is only deadly if it is accessed and used accordingly. When we use it, we have to believe it will work. Otherwise, we are shooting spiritual blanks when we pray without faith.

DAY 20

THE POWER OF PRAYER COMES FROM THE GOD TO WHOM WE PRAY

In 1 Kings 18:20-40, the prophet Elijah confronts the prophets of Baal at Mount Carmel. Elijah challenges the prophets of Baal to a contest because he was fed up with the Israelites who were worshipping both God and Baal. In verse 21, *Elijah came near to all the people and said, how long will you go limping between two different opinions? If the Lord is God, follow Him; but if Baal, then follow Him.*

Elijah asked the people to take two bulls. One of the bulls was given to the prophets of Baal. He told them to put the bull on a pile of wood and put no fire to it (v. 23). Then he took the other bull and put it on a pile of wood without fire. The prophets of Baal prayed to their gods for fire to fall on their bull, but nothing happened. However, Elijah prayed to the God of Abraham, Isaac and Israel, then the fire of the Lord fell and consumed the bull (v. 38).

The point here is the prayer of the prophets of Baal had no power because their god was an idol. However, Elijah's prayer was effective because he prayed to the Omnipotent God, who is the creator of all things. Elijah won the contest because he called on the name of the Lord.

The power of prayer is in the God to whom we pray. Let us not forget, the God who invites us to pray *is able to do exceedingly and more* *abundantly than we can ask or imagine* (Ephesians 3:22). When we go to the Lord in prayer in the name of Jesus, we can be confident our prayer will be dynamic in its impact.

Whenever we access God's throne of grace through prayer, we also open ourselves to all of God's Heavenly blessings. No one enters into a fellowship of prayer with God and walks away without a blessing. *In the presence of God is the fullness of joy* (Psalm 16:11).

QUESTIONS FOR SELF REFLECTION

THE POWER OF PRAYER COMES FROM THE GOD TO WHOM WE PRAY

(1 Kings 18:20-40)

What is the source of Elijah's confidence in competing against the prophets of Baal?

He Know the power of prayer

Why do you think the prophets of Baal could not get their god to light up the fire?

He was praying to an idol God

To whom did Elijah pray to light up the fire, after he poured water on the wood three times? The God of Abraham, Isaac, and Israel

He prayeth to Omnipotent God who is the creator of all things

What did Elijah say in his prayer?

How can your prayer be as powerful as Elijah's prayer?

When we Go to God in the name of Jesus we can be confident our prayers will be powerful & impactful.

DAY 21

THE POWER OF PRAYER IS IN THE HOLY SPIRIT WHO INTERCEDES FOR US

Romans 8:26, reminds us that we do not know how to pray. The Holy Spirit himself intercedes for us through wordless groans. It is precisely because the Holy Spirit is interceding for us that prayer is so powerful. The Holy Spirit is our counselor, our intercessor, and our enabler.

The Holy Spirit is the third Person in the Triune God. He is omnipotent in His power, omnipresent in His outreach, and omniscient in His intercession. No one or nothing can prevent the Holy Spirit from fulfilling His purpose on our behalf.

Having the Holy Spirit interceding for us means our prayer is guaranteed to get to the Father. This does not mean we always get the answer we desire. However, we can be confident the outcome of a prayer, "in the name of Jesus" will work to our good.

This then is why the God to whom we pray is so important. The Holy Spirit is only going to intercede for us if we pray to the Triune God of heaven. He will not be involved in any prayer to an idol or to any other god. For example, we should not expect the Spirit to intercede for anyone who prays to Buddha. The Holy Spirit is greater than Buddha. He is not in fellowship with Buddha.

Notice, the Holy Spirit did not intercede for the prophets of Baal in their contest with Elijah. He did however intercede for Elijah who defeated the prophets of Baal and killed 450 of them. Without the Holy Spirit's intercession, a prayer is but an empty request that spiritual powers and principalities can easily hinder.

The Holy Spirit makes it impossible for spiritual powers and principalities to interfere with our petitions as they did in Daniel 10. He is the Third Person in the Triune Godhead. No evil force can challenge the Holy Spirit. That is why the Holy Spirit guarantees a divine response to every prayer in the name of Jesus—though we may not appreciate the response.

It was by the power of the Holy Spirit that the spiritual organism called the Church was established, after the disciples met in the upper room to pray. Everything the saints did in the New Testament church was through prayer because they were led by the Holy Spirit. That same Spirit set Peter free from prison while the church was praying for him (Acts 12:1-18).

Jesus knew we would not be able to break through the spiritual interference we experience to get our prayer to God. He also knew we would not know the right thing to say during prayer, and that our prayer would be impotent because of our sinful nature. That is why He gave us the Holy Spirit.

The Holy Spirit seals the presence of Jesus Christ in the heart of the believer. Therefore, we can come boldly before our Father in Heaven through prayer, so that we may receive mercy and find grace to help us in our time of need (Hebrews 11:6). It is the Holy Spirit, who leads us to God's throne and guarantees the efficacy of our intercession.

The language of prayer is a language of power because it involves the Holy Spirit. When my children really want something from me, they go to their mother first and ask her to come ask me on their behalf. When their mother comes to me on their behalf, she does so with all the rights and privileges afforded to her as my wife. It is indeed far more difficult for me to say no to my wife than it is to say no to my children.

Using my wife as their advocate, makes the petition of my children more meaningful and effectual because I trust my wife will make sure what they are requesting will be to their personal and spiritual benefit. When my children come to me on their own, I often ask if they talked to their mom first. Without their mother's intercession, their petition is tabled for discussion and evaluation until such a time as I feel confident they really need what they request, and they will be responsible stewards when their request is granted.

The Father trusts that whenever the Holy Spirit intercedes for us it is worth His attention. He knows the Holy Spirit will never bring requests before Him that is not in line with the Father's will for our lives. As the Third Person in the Triune Godhead, the Holy Spirit has all the rights and privilege to come to the Father on our behalf with the confidence that the Father will listen and act accordingly.

QUESTIONS FOR SELF REFLECTION

THE POWER OF PRAYER IS IN THE HOLY SPIRIT WHO INTERCEDES FOR US

(Romans 8:26-27)

How does the Holy Spirit intercede for believers?

Through wordless groans

How does the Holy Spirit make our prayer powerful and effective?

He is omnipotent in His power, omnipresent in His outreach, and omniscient in His intercession on our behalf.

What does it mean to have the Holy Spirit make intercession for us?

It means our prayer is guaranteed to get to the Father and will work for our good.

Why were the disciples empowered by the Holy Spirit to speak in tongues on the Day of Pentecost?

____

____

____

Why do you think the Church cannot do the Great Commission without the Holy Spirit?

The Holy Spirit seals the presence of Jesus Christ in the hearts of believers.

DAY 22

THE POWER OF PRAYER HAS A LOT TO DO WITH THE ATTITUDE WITH WHICH WE PRAY

The Holy Spirit will only intercede for those who pray with an attitude of faith. Jesus taught us that effectual prayer requires faith. Faith is like the bullets in a revolver. Without the bullets, the revolver is just a funny-shaped piece of metal. It would not be able to do any physical harm. Criminals would not be afraid of police officers.

In the same way, spiritual powers and principalities are not afraid of prayers lacking in faith. It is our faith in God, through Jesus Christ, that makes our prayer spiritually lethal to the forces of evil. Faith is like a spiritual password that gives us access to God's throne of grace through prayer.

It does not matter the size of the faith to be the beneficiary of divine miracles. What is necessary, is for the petitioner to believe that God can do what he or she is asking to be done. In Matthew 17:20, Jesus reassured us that all it take is faith the size of a mustard seed for mountain moving miracles to occur on our behalf.

The potency of our prayer depends on the vitality of our faith. People who believe they can *do all things through Christ who strengthens them* tend to be more focused, determined, and hopeful in the pursuit of their desires. Though they are knocked down, they always find the strength to bounce back and move forward toward their goal. These faith-based Christians tend to pray with a spirit of expectation that makes it very difficult for them to feel defeated.

When we pray with earnest faith, we demolish spiritual strongholds, and are able to walk in the fullness of God's purpose for our lives. A faith-based prayer is covered with Holy Ghost fire and resistant to all forms of demonic attack. Such prayer is like a sweet smelling offering to God that Revelation 8:4-5 tells us will fill the censer with fire from the altar of God.

Praying with an attitude of worship accentuates the power of prayer. Whenever we set out to worship Almighty God, we invite the angelic hosts to participate. That invitation takes prayer to a Heavenly realm and makes it a spiritual act that is impervious to demonic interference.

Worship sets the atmosphere for the fullness of God's glory to be revealed. Prayerful worship makes us aware of the presence of God and gives us a greater love for God, which makes us serve the Almighty with zeal and determination. An attitude of worship leads to a life of spiritual consecration. Such a consecrated life is informed by the Holy Spirit and is lived out with audacious faith.

Prayerful worship helps us to let go of our fears and commune with God with a spirit of expectation. Worship aligns our petition with the Spirit of truth and makes our interaction with God more meaningful and spiritually fulfilling. Furthermore, worship indicates that we are more concerned about reverencing God rather than the blessings He offers. It also suggests that we acknowledge the power of God to do more abundantly than we can ask or imagine. Thus, we become confident that everything will work or our good, no matter how God chooses to answer our prayer.

QUESTIONS FOR SELF REFLECTION

THE POWER OF PRAYER HAS TO DO WITH THE ATTITUDE WITH WHICH WE PRAY

(Matthew 17:20)

What attitude should believers have when praying?

We should have a faith attitude knowing God will hear and answer prayers.

What are the benefits of praying with an attitude of worship?

Worship accentuates the power of prayer, angelic host participate, it sets the atmosphere for the fullness of God's glory to be revealed, were are aware of His presence

Define an attitude of faith. Why is an attitude of faith necessary in prayer?

Attitude of faith is believing and knowing you receive. It's necessary because it makes our prayer spiritually lethal to the forces of evil

What does an attitude of faith say about our relationship with God?

It Say we trust God

What does prayerful worship indicate?

We reverence God and exault Him
gives us a greater love for Him
and we're aware of His presence

DAY 23

THE POWER OF PRAYER IS IN THE LANGUAGE WITH WHICH WE PRAY.

Proverbs 18:21 tells us, *the tongue has the power of life and death.* **We should never underestimate the power of our words.** In Genesis 1, we read that God spoke the world into existence. Human beings are the only creature God did not speak into being. Instead, He physically took clay from the ground to shape us. Then He blew His spirit into us.

The Bible gives us the vocabulary to pray with authority. Too many prayers are invalidated because of the language used by the supplicant. When we use words that are Spirit-led we increase the efficacy of our prayer. That is why it is necessary to pray according to Scripture.

When we use the language of God (the Bible) to pray to God, we monopolize the attention of the Almighty, and we can expect Him to move on our behalf. Jesus warned His disciples not to babble during prayer. Instead, He cautioned them to be strategic with their words (Matthew 6:7). I think this is because, every careless word we use can be detrimental to the spiritual connection we try to make with God during prayer.

The word of the believer is so powerful that Jesus said on two occasions in the Gospel of Matthew, *Whatever you bind on earth will be bound in heaven, and whatever you loose on earth will be loosed in heaven*

(Matthew 16:18-19; 18:18-19). This is a confirmation of how powerful our prayer can be because of the language we use. The powerful language of prayer can be used to wage spiritual warfare against powers and principalities in high places.

When Jesus sent out His disciples two by two in Luke 10, He told them exactly what they should say during their missionary journey. To the disciples' amazement, even the demons submitted to them because they said and did what Jesus told them to do. It is wise for believers to ask the Holy Spirit for the words they should say during prayer. When believers pray the words of scripture, or repeat what the Holy Spirit tells them, their prayer is undeniably potent.

There are some words we should not use when communicating with God. We should never say: "If you," "then I." This suggests it is to God's benefit to do what we are asking Him to do. Let us not forget, God does not need anything from us. He is self-sufficient. I cringe when I hear people say during their prayer. For example, "If you do all these things, we will give you glory and honor."

God does not have to earn our glory and honor. The angels in Heaven are glorifying Him around the clock. The stars, the sun, and the moon stand in awe of Him. Whether or not I glorify God is not going to lessen His Divinity or impact His Sovereignty. Besides, God should be praised in the good and the not so good. We should praise God when our blessings are delayed or denied.

We need to change our way of speaking. Instead, we should say, "When you do all these things, I will tell everyone that you alone did them, so your name can be praised all the more." Believers should not forget demonic spirits are also listening to the words we speak. Whereas they cannot read our mind or know our intentions, they can hear our words. Our duty is to let these demonic spirits know we will praise God in all circumstances.

It is not wise to say "If God does not answer my prayer, I will never pray or believe in the existence of God." Again, God is not obligated to answer our wishes; He is not a genie. We cannot give God an ultimatum. When God did not answer David's prayer to heal his first child with Bathsheba, David worshipped God anyway.

We curse ourselves when we give God an ultimatum. The Holy

Spirit cannot and will not intercede on behalf of an ultimatum. All ultimatums are dead before they even get to the altar of God's grace.

We should also not say, "Why do you bless so and so, but you are not answering my prayer?" This is the language of jealousy and envy, which is also dead on arrival. God knows what He is doing. His purpose for us may not be the same as for our neighbor, colleague, or family member. This sort of prayer is designed to establish blame and not to find grace.

In Matthew 12:36, Jesus told the disciples, *But, I tell* you *that everyone will have to give account on the day of judgment for every careless word they have spoken*. This is not an idle threat. It is a reminder of the power of words. At times I find myself telling God that I don't know what to say in prayer. So I begin by asking for the Lord to edify my words, so my prayer can be acceptable in His sight.

Before we start praying, we should meditate and think long and hard about the things we are going to say. At times, it is best to remain silent inside and outside of ourselves in a spirit of meditation, instead of saying empty words in prayer. A wise person knows when to speak, what to say, and how much to say. Careful words in prayer are like music to the Lord's ears.

The words we speak determine the life we live. Paul told the saints at Ephesus to avoid obscene language and foolish talk because they do not edify the soul. Our spiritual enemy is looking for any opportunity to poison our spirit and send us on the path of self-destruction. Our prayer should always be, *Let the words of our mouths and the meditation of our hearts be acceptable in your sight, oh Lord, my strength, and my redeemer* (Psalm 19:14).

QUESTIONS FOR SELF REFLECTION

THE POWER OF PRAYER HAS TO DO WITH THE LANGUAGE WITH WHICH WE PRAY

(Matthew 16:18-19; 18:18-19)

What is the language of God?

The Scripture -

What are the benefits in praying with the language of God?

What words should the believer not use when praying?

What are the consequences of speaking unwisely in prayer?

____

____

____

Where can we find the right words to pray?

____

____

____

CONCLUSION

Anyone who has experienced a genuine conversion, and has faith in God through Jesus Christ knows about the power of prayer. The power of prayer is not something that can be taught; it must be experienced. The only way to know about the power of prayer is to pray earnestly and fervently.

One thing I know for sure, I am a living and walking example of the power of prayer. I am alive today because of the power of prayer. The more I pray, the stronger I become in my spiritual warfare against the enemy.

The power of prayer keeps demons away from the people of God. Fervent prayer is a repellant to demonic spirits. When a husband and wife pray for each other, demonic spirits stay out of their marriage. Also, their children are blessed, and peace and harmony dwell in the house because the Spirit of God abides therein.

We should pray before making any important decision. Prayer is both a defensive and an offensive weapon. We should not wait to pray when things go bad. Prayer should saturate our thinking, so that we may be discerning in our judgment.

Most of the bad decisions I have made are because I did not pray before making those decisions. I am convinced when I pray before making a decision God will correct my thinking and prepare me for the outcome of my prayer. Prayer helps us to see things from God's perspective. While we are trying to wait on God to sort things out for us, prayer will keep our spiritual enemy from interfering in our affairs.

SMALL GROUP DISCUSSION

THE POWER OF PRAYER

The Question: What is the Power of Prayer?
The Point: The Prayer of a righteous person is powerful and effective.

Background Passage: James 5:13-18
Lesson Passage: James 5:16
Memory Verse: James 5:16

Introduction

The Bible instructs us to pray fervently because our prayers work. There are countless stories in the Old and New Testament about the power of prayer. Yet, the question remains, "What type of power is there in prayer?" The answer depends on the need and the faith of the individual. Indeed, the power of prayer is faith based.

In Matthew 21:22, Jesus told the disciples, *you can pray for anything, and if you have faith, you will receive it.* A faithless prayer is weak and dead on arrival. A faith-based prayer is powerful enough to raise a person from the dead. In Matthew 14:29, Peter began to walk on water because he had faith. As soon as his faith waivered, he began to sink, such that Jesus had to rescue him. However, in Acts 9:40 that same Peter raised Tabitha from the dead through the power of prayer because his faith had increased.

Background/Context

Faith is the natural language with which the Church of Jesus Christ communicates its mission. Because of this faith, the prayer of those in the Body of Christ is inherently powerful. Thus, if any member of the church is in trouble, that person is to pray. James reminded believers, *If anyone among them was sick, they were to call the elders of the church to pray over them and anoint them with oil in the name of the Lord (5:14).*

The exhortation from James is consistent with Old Testament practices wherein a Jew was to go to the rabbi to be anointed with oil when sick, instead of a doctor. Then the rabbi would pray over the sick person. In the early church, the elders took on the role of rabbis. They were to be men of faith whose prayer could heal the sick. The instruction from James presupposes the power of healing was prevalent in the early church because it was a praying church.

James notion that the prayer of a righteous person is powerful and effective (5:16) highlights a key theological point. A person must be made righteous through Christ for their prayer to be powerful and effective. This is why the believer prays in Jesus' name. The power of prayer does not come from us. It originates and resides with the Lord, Jesus Christ. Therefore, through prayer, *we can heal the sick, raise the dead, and set the captives free, in the name of Jesus* (Matthew 10:8).

QUESTIONS FOR SMALL GROUP DISCUSSION

What makes prayer powerful?

Faith

If the prayer of the righteous person is powerful and effective, why doesn't all prayer work?

Wrong Motives

What do you do when your prayer is not powerful and effective enough to get the desired answer?

What role does faith play in making prayer powerful and effective?

What is the significance of anointing people with holy oil?

PRAYER TIPS FOR THIS CHAPTER

Understand you have the power to change outcomes and circumstances when you pray. Go into the prayer exercise with confidence and a spirit of expectation. Exercise faith and trust in God's omnipotence and providential love, no matter the gravity of your circumstance. Use biblical texts that reference the power of prayer to encourage your spirit when you pray.

Life Application Questions

1. How is Mark 11:24 influencing your prayer life?
2. What does it mean to intercede for others in prayer?
3. What is your attitude when you pray?
4. What language do you use when you pray?

Sample Prayer

Blessed Lord, grant me the faith to set the captives free, heal the sick, and bind demonic spirits through the fervency of my prayers.

Please let me not grow faint in my spiritual warfare with the enemy as I use the weapon of prayer to tear down every spiritual stronghold in the name of Jesus. Give me the confidence to pray with a spirit of expectancy knowing that the earnest prayer of a righteous person has great power and produces wonderful results (James 5:16).

CHAPTER V

THE DIFFERENT TYPES OF PRAYER

When Solomon had finished the temple of the Lord and the royal palace, and had succeeded in carrying out all he had in mind to do in the temple of the Lord and in his own palace, the Lord appeared to him at night and said: "I have heard your prayer and have chosen this place for myself as a temple for sacrifices. "When I shut up the heavens so that there is no rain, or command locusts to devour the land or send a plague among my people, if my people, who are called by my name, will humble themselves and pray and seek my face and turn from their wicked ways, then I will hear from heaven, and I will forgive their sin and will heal their land. 2 Chronicles 7:14

It is necessary to learn about the different types of prayer in order to pray more effectively. As children of God, we have to know the type of language we are using when talking to Him. That makes our conversation more relevant and specific.

I think people tend to use more clichés and vain repetitions while praying because they do not understand the different types of prayer. For example, one should not be confusing prayer of intercession with prayer of invocation. When asked to pray for others or at a public gathering, one has to know the type of prayer appropriate for the occasion.

It is **not** necessary to know the different types of prayer for personal devotional. Indeed, during our individual prayer time, we can mix and match prayer types at will. However, as members of the body of Christ, we are also call to pray in community with others. Therefore, we have to know the different types of prayer so we can pray as requested by others. That is particularly relevant for people who are called to five-fold ministry.

This chapter focuses on the nine main types of prayer discussed in the Bible: (1) prayer of faith (see James 5:15); (2) prayer of supplication (Philippians 4:16; (3) prayer of petition or intercession (John 17:6-26); (4) prayer of thanksgiving (Psalm 69:30); (5) prayer of adoration (Acts 13:2-3); (6) prayer of consecration and dedication (2 Chronicles 6:12-40); (7) prayer of lament (Psalm 69); (8) prayer of meditation (Joshua 1:8); and (9) Mercy Prayer (Psalm 4:1; 6:2; 9:13; 28:2; Hebrews 4:16).

DAY 24

PRAYER OF FAITH (JAMES 5:15)

In James 5:15, we read, *and the prayer offered in faith will make the sick person well; the Lord will raise them up. If they have sinned, they will be forgiven.* Previously in Chapter IV, a section was devoted to praying with the attitude of faith.

What does a prayer of faith look like? It is praying with a spirit of expectation that I refer to as "Spiritual Assumption." It is assuming we already have what we are requesting. This does not mean God is obligated to grant our petitions. It is based on the belief that God always answers prayer, one way or another. The answer could be "Yes," "No," or "Wait." However, we always get an answer.

Such a prayer requires trust in the Word of God, and total confidence in His promises. This prayer of faith is based on the conviction that nothing is impossible with God. That assumption requires total dependency on God, and a willingness to wait patiently on the Lord and be of good courage (Psalm 27:14).

Without faith, prayer is an exercise in futility. Our faith in God causes the Holy Spirit to intercede on our behalf. Besides, how can people pray to a deity in whom they do not believe? Only by faith can we commune with God in the spirit. The Spirit of God only understands the language of faith. Faith in whom? It is faith in the Triune God—Father, Son, and Holy Spirit.

We all have faith in something. Followers of other religions have faith in their gods. However, followers of Jesus Christ have faith in the God who sent His Son to die for the salvation of His creation. The Christian claim is there is only One God, who is above all and in all. This God became flesh in the person of Jesus Christ. Therefore, we should put our faith in this God!

Our faith must be resilient and stubborn. At times, we may have to wait a while before our prayer is answered. However, Jesus teaches that we should keep asking until we get what we ask. It takes faith and spiritual stubbornness to keep praying and expecting God to answer. Faith prayer is not for the faint-hearted.

If you always get an answer how can answer be NO?

Should we keep asking or continue to thank Him for answered prayer.

QUESTIONS FOR SELF REFLECTION

PRAYER OF FAITH

(James 5:15)

What is "Spiritual Assumption" in prayer?

Praying with expectation of answered prayer

What it the purpose of a prayer of faith?

How do we distinguish between a prayer of faith and the other types of prayer? Give an example.

Prayer of faith is total dependency on God – where as other prayer

What did Jesus say about praying in faith?

What are the two things required for a prayer of faith?

Faith in the Triune God

Resilient and Stubborn faith

DAY 25

PRAYER OF SUPPLICATION

In Philippians 4:16, Paul told the saints of Philippi, *Do not be anxious about anything, but in every situation, by prayer and petition, with thanksgiving, present your requests to God.*

A prayer of supplication is asking God for something. It is a request from the person praying. In the Bible, the word supplication comes from the Hebrew and Greek word that means "a request or petition."

Prayers of supplication and petition are similar in character because they are both requests. However, the difference is who is the recipient of the prayer. A prayer of petition is a request on behalf of others, while a prayer of supplication is request on behalf of self.

A prayer of supplication requires faith. It is not necessarily a prayer of desperation. It is a request for a personal need that is often urgent, and comes from a heart crying out to God. There are numerous examples of prayer of supplication in the Bible. Psalm 4:1; Psalm 5:8; Psalm 6:4; Psalm 7:1, are prayers of supplication by David. In the New Testament, Paul told the saints at Ephesus to make supplications for all the saints (Ephesians 6:8).

A prayer of supplication is a form of intercession. The only difference is intercession is always done on behalf of others. I will devote an entire section for intercession below.

Our supplication to God is not begging. We use prayer of supplication to unload our burdens to the Lord. It comes from a place of intimacy with God. Paul offered a prayer of supplication to God in 2 Corinthians 12:8-9. Though he did not get the answer he was hoping for, he learned about the sufficiency of God's grace. Subsequently, he was able to rejoice in his weakness because of his trust in the Lord.

QUESTIONS FOR SELF REFLECTION

PRAYER OF SUPPLICATION

(Philippians 4:16)

What is the purpose of a prayer of supplication?

To ask God for something

When should we pray a prayer of supplication?

When you have an urgent Need

What is required to pray a prayer of supplication?

Faith is required

What is the difference between begging and a prayer of supplication?

Supplication is a request, you unload a burden onto the Lord

What is the relationship between spiritual supplication and intercession?

Supplication is a form of intercession

DAY 26

PRAYER OF PETITION OR INTERCESSION

When we petition God on behalf of others, our request is called intercession. The Word of God instructs believers to pray for one another. Intercession can be done individually or communally. Through intercessory prayer, we accept God's invitation to intervene spiritually for a brother or sister in their hour of need. "Intercession is God's brilliant strategy for including the saints in ruling with Him in power." (Rebecca Jordan). When we intercede for others we partner with them in the spirit to release the power of our faith for a positive outcome.

Intercession unites our hearts to people and places we pray for. Unity of the spirit is a formidable spiritual weapon. The idea of praying for others implies self-sacrificial love. It highlights our desire to consider the needs of others as more significant than our needs. This also demonstrates a desire to not only look to our own interests, but also to the interests of others (Philippians 2:3-4 ESV).

Intercession renews our hope and faith. When we intercede for others, this renews our hope and faith in God and in one another. At times, all we can offer our neighbor, in their hour of need, is the hope we will cry out to God on their behalf. The idea that other people are interceding on our behalf, gives us hope and renews our faith as we await the deliverance of the Lord.

Intercession makes a long-term impact beyond this age. Many people are saved because someone prayed for them. Before the ascension of Jesus, He interceded for His disciples and for all believers in John 17:6-26. Because of that prayer of intercession, followers of Jesus Christ are able to do the work of ministry. This work will transform this earthly kingdom into the kingdom of God.

When we intercede on behalf of the unsaved, we partner with God to bring about a bountiful spiritual harvest for His eternal kingdom. My mother prayed for me from infancy. Her prayer of intercession encouraged me to serve the Lord with all of my heart and soul. There have been times when I wanted to quit pastoral ministry. However, every time I think about my mother's intercession on my behalf, I become encouraged and more determined to do the Lord's will.

Intercessory prayer changes the atmosphere in homes, relationships, cities, nations, and churches. I had a man from my church who asked me what he could do to strengthen his failing marriage. I advised him to start praying for his wife and let her hear him praying for her. Two weeks later, he came back and told me how praying for his wife invigorated his marriage.

The fact is that when family members intercede for one another it creates an atmosphere of peace and love in their relationship and brings forth harmony in the home. In 1 Timothy 2:1-2, the writer says, *First of all, I urge that petitions, prayers, intercession, and thanksgiving be offered on behalf of all people—for kings and all those in authority, so that we may lead tranquil and quiet lives in all godliness and dignity.*

Church members should pray for one another because the Church of Jesus Christ is forever under spiritual attack. We should intercede for political leaders, business leaders, teachers, pastors, and all others in position of leadership, so that they can make wise decisions as influencers. God will only heal our land from gun violence, endemic racism, and the proliferation of structural injustice when believers make intercessions unto the Lord.

Luke tells us to *Give, and it will be given to you. A good measure, pressed down, shaken together and running over, will be poured into your lap. For with the measure you use, it will be measured to you* (Luke 6:38). Simply stated: intercession causes multiple blessings to return to the intercessor.

As we intercede for others in prayer, we will receive overflowing blessings from the Lord. The Lord will also reward the intercessor for his or her faithfulness, kindness and compassion in taking the time to intercede on behalf of someone else. We do show the heart of Christ when we spend time interceding for others. The heart of Christ is pleasing to God. It serenades the Almighty and causes an automatic reaction of overflow favor from the Almighty to shower upon the intercessor.

QUESTIONS FOR SELF REFLECTION

PRAY OF PETITION OR INTERCESSION

(John 17:6-26)

What are the two ways we can make intercession?

____

____

____

What happens during a prayer of intercession?

____

____

____

Describe the impact of prayer of intercession.

____

____

____

For whom should we intercede?

___

___

___

What are the personal benefits of interceding for others?

___

___

___

DAY 27

PRAYER OF THANKSGIVING

Some people only think about prayer of thanksgiving on Thanksgiving Day (Fourth Thursday of November in the US). It is as if that is the only day people should thank God for His unfailing love and providential care. Even on Thanksgiving Day, the focus is often on the food—turkey and all the fixings—and not on a genuine spirit of thanksgiving to God. A prayer of thanksgiving is a special moment to celebrate God's faithfulness to us. Thanksgiving is always accompanied with praise and worship.

During a prayer of thanksgiving, the individual focuses solely on thanking God without making any petition or supplication. In Psalm 69:30, the Psalmist declares, *I will praise God's name in song and glorify him with thanksgiving*. The expression of thanksgiving in prayer sets the atmosphere for praise and worship. One cannot commune with God with a heart of thanksgiving without being prompted to praise His Holiness.

It is a good practice to set aside one day of the week, or one prayer session per day to offer thanksgiving to God. Johnson Oatman, Jr. wrote in the hymn entitled "Count Your Blessings,"

When upon life's billows you are tempest-tossed,

When you are discouraged, thinking all is lost,
Count your many blessings, name them one by one,
And it will surprise you what the Lord has done.

A PRAYER OF THANKSGIVING IS ABOUT COUNTING OUR MANY BLESSINGS, notwithstanding the storms we may be facing currently. On Thanksgiving Day, people are expected to count their blessings and name them so others can know what God has done for them. Unfortunately, most people tend to forget all the things God has done for them throughout the year by the time they get to Thanksgiving Day. That is why it is necessary to devote time in prayer to thank God at least once per week.

During prayer of thanksgiving we are compelled to provide a justification as to why we are thanking God. The heavens and the angelic hosts wants to hear why we are thanking God. Psalm 136 provides every Christian with a biblically sound reason for giving thanks to God in prayer: *For he is good.* Psalm 136 is called a Psalm of Great Praise in Jewish tradition for the way it rehearses God's goodness regarding His people and encourages them to praise Him for His merciful and steadfast love. (James Montgomery Boice)

Many people find it challenging to focus their minds to pray. Some readily admit the reason they do not pray is because they do not know what to say. These same individuals would often offer impromptu thanksgiving to God for different reasons. A prayer of thanksgiving provides the opportunity and the language to pray. All a person has to say is "thank you Lord for so and so."

QUESTIONS FOR SELF REFLECTION

PRAYER OF THANKSGIVING

(Psalm 69:30)

When should we pray a prayer of thanksgiving?

Daily

What happens during a prayer of thanksgiving?

Give thank to God, for what He's done and what He's going to do.

Why is it necessary to offer prayer of thanksgiving?

What reason is provided in Psalm 136 for believers to offer thanksgiving to God?

What are the benefits for offering a prayer of thanksgiving?

DAY 28

PRAYER OF ADORATION

Whereas prayer is an act of worship, there is a specific type of prayer whose sole purpose is to worship. In Acts 13:2-3 we read, *While they were worshipping the Lord and fasting, the Holy Spirit said, "Set apart for me Barnabas and Saul for the work to which I have called them. So after they had fasted and prayed, they placed their hands on them and sent them off.*

A prayer of adoration offers the space for the individual to exalt the name of the Lord. It is a time to contemplate the Holiness of God and to worship His sovereignty. At least once a week, I set time aside to worship God in prayer. For about 20 to 30 minutes, I instruct my soul to magnify the Lord. During this time, I focus on the majesty of God and celebrate His faithful love for me. It helps me become more aware of the significance of Jesus' death at the cross and His gift of salvation.

A prayer of adoration always includes thanksgiving for our redemption through Jesus Christ. It must contain thanksgiving for God's amazing grace. When the leaders of the Church at Antioch met to pray, they worshipped God for saving Gentiles like them. They were fasting and praying to deepen their experience of the presence of God. It was during such a time of prayerful worship that the Holy Spirit asked them to *Set apart for me Barnabas and Saul for the work to which I have called them.*

There is something special about communing with God in prayer with worship as the only item on the agenda. This is precisely what the church leaders at Antioch were doing in Acts 13:2-3 that prompted the Holy Spirit to show up. The fact that they were fasting while praying, intensified their worship experience and made their prayer more effectual.

In today's church services, prayer of adoration is often used as invocation. A prayer of invocation is offered at the opening of a church service or Christian ceremony to invoke God's blessings over the worship service. It is an invitation for the Holy Spirit to participate in, take control of, and delight in the worship of the Triune God.

In Luke 1:46-56, we have a good example of a prayer of adoration offered by Mary, the mother of Jesus. When Elizabeth greeted Mary and told her how honored she was to have the mother of the Lord visit her, Mary said:

My soul glorifies the Lord and my spirit rejoices in God my Savior,
for He has been mindful of the humble state of his servant.
From now on all generations will call me blessed, for the Mighty One has
done great things for me—holy is His name. His mercy extends
to those who fear Him, from generation to generation.
He has performed mighty deeds with His arm; He has scattered
those who are proud in their inmost thoughts. He has brought down
from their thrones but has lifted up the humble. He has filled the hungry
with good things but has sent the rich away empty. He has helped
His servant Israel, remembering to be merciful to Abraham and His
descendants forever, just as He promised our ancestors.

This portion of scripture is called The Magnificat. It is a combined prayer, poem, and hymn of praise. Mary was so overwhelmed with joy that she worshipped the Lord and earnestly conveyed her gratitude to Almighty God in a prayer of worship.

QUESTIONS FOR SELF REFLECTION

PRAYER OF ADORATION

(Acts 13:2-3)

What is a prayer of adoration?

One that offers space for the individual to exault the name of the Lord

What are the components of a prayer of adoration?

Worship, thanksgiving

What is a prayer of invocation?

One to invoke God's Blessings over a worship Service - inviting the Holy Spirit to take Control

When is a prayer of invocation offered?

Church Svc
Christian Ceremony

What is special about Mary's prayer of worship in Luke 1:46-56?

Prayer of adoration by Elizabeth for
being in the presence of Jesus' mom
Mary

DAY 29

PRAYER OF CONSECRATION AND DEDICATION

Throughout the Christian journey, the believer will experience spiritual recession. A country experiences recession when the economy declines significantly for at least six months. Believers can experience spiritual recession when their passion for worship is waning, their commitment to prayer is declining, their interest in the Word of God is weakening, or their longing for fellowship with God and other believers is fading.

Spiritual recession occurs when believers forsake their first love for God. Consequently, they move away from the Almighty, and stop sensing His presence the way they once did. During a spiritual recession, the person loses their hunger for God and stop prioritizing the things of God over the things of this world. It is at that point they need to be consecrated.

Through a prayer of consecration, the believer aims to recommit their life to God. Recommitment begins with repenting for allowing their spirit to become disinterested in God and the things of God. It requires confession, and closes with a petition for the Holy Spirit to restore the joy of salvation for that person.

Psalm 51 contains many of the characteristics of a prayer of consecration. It includes the following:

1. A Confession
2. A plea for Mercy
3. A desire for holiness
4. An acknowledgment of the greatness of God
5. A Doxology

The word consecration literally mean "association with the sacred." In the Old Testament, the people of Israel were consecrated unto God, as well as, the kings, the priests and the prophets. Consecration in the Bible is the sincere dedication to a special purpose or service. It is also known as anointing.

During all ordination services, a prayer of consecration is offered to God on behalf of the person who is being ordained. In that prayer we ask God to sanctify the person so his or her steps can be ordered by God. We also ask for God to fan the flame of the Holy Spirit in the person's heart so they can bear spiritual fruits for the kingdom of God.

In the Baptist faith tradition, babies are dedicated or consecrated to God. The parents are obligated to dedicate their child to the Lord. In the Old Testament, Hannah dedicated Samuel to the Lord. Samson was also dedicated to the Lord. A prayer of dedication, therefore, is a surrender of the spiritual gifting of a person, or a thing, or ministry to God for the sole purpose of His kingdom building work on earth. It is a formal declaration of one's intent to consecrate someone or something to God.

QUESTIONS FOR SELF REFLECTION

PRAYER OF CONSECRATION AND DEDICATION

(2 Chronicles 6:12-40)

What is a prayer of consecration?

Recommittment to God

What is a prayer of dedication?

Surrender of Spiritual gifting of a person or ministry to God for His Kingdom work on earth

What are the characteristics of a prayer of consecration?

Ask God to Sanctify the person so their steps are ordered by God.

Why should Christian parents dedicate their children?

When do we consecrate people in the Christian Church?

DAY 30

PAYER OF LAMENT

A lament is a passionate expression of grief or sorrow. A prayer of lament is used to petition God for help in a situation of distress, suffering, and hardship. It is used to ask God to intervene urgently on behalf of the person who is suffering.

Prayer of lament originates from a heart of sorrow and a soul in need of divine deliverance. The Hebrew Psalter contains many prayers of lament. By some estimate, at least 70 percent of the Psalms are laments. The book of Lamentations is said to be one long prayer of lament.

During a prayer of lament, the supplicant cries out to God. He or she is often moved to tears as they express their need to God. Those emotional tears often compel the supplicant to use frank language without any desire for formality or platitudes. There is often a sense of anger and resentment toward God for failing to intervene and prevent the situation from worsening.

Those cries are also sent forth in frustration because the supplicant believes God has the power to deliver, yet they struggle to comprehend why their deliverance is delayed. There is also a sense that lamenting one's condition by crying out to God is therapeutic.

In Psalm 69, David says, *I am worn out calling for help; my throat is parched. My eyes fail, looking for God.* He was emotionally exhausted from crying out to God. In the midst of his lament, he asks for the salvation of the Lord to protect him (v 29).

A prayer of lament is intended to ask for help in difficult times. It is only offered when the supplicant needs God's help to deal with a difficult situation. David often prayed in lament to ask God for help against his enemies. Many of his prayers of lament were uttered while he was running away from King Saul who wanted to kill him.

There will be times when the believer laments their condition amidst the silence of God. I have had to lament my circumstance to God in prayer on several occasions. God invites us to ask for His help. He does not frown upon those who question His benevolence in the midst of their storms.

We do not always know what God is doing, or how long it is going to take the Lord to deliver us. When the pressure is too much to endure, or our soul is overwhelmed with a situation that is beyond our control, we are naturally prone to ask God for help. The challenge then is for us to be able to wait on God to deliver us.

As believers, we know our help comes from the Lord, who made heaven and earth (Psalm 121: 1-2). However, we would be disingenuous to say we do not lament to God in prayer when our faith is tested, and our patience is tried by the trials of life. Our natural tendency is to run to God for help when trouble like sea billows roll into our lives.

There is a second challenge fundamental to our prayer life in times of sorrow and grief. It is the challenge to express our sorrow or grief to the Almighty with spiritual integrity while showing reverence to His Sovereignty. The question then is how do we lament our circumstance to God in prayer while fanning the flame of our faith in His providential love?

In truth, it is difficult to pray any other type of prayer when our soul is vexed by the vicissitudes of life. Whether we know it or not, the type of prayer we pray is influenced by our existential reality. Seldom do people offer prayer of thanksgiving or intercession when they have an urgent self-need they want God to address. And, that's okay because God wants us to commune with Him in Spirit and in truth.

Since He already knows what is in our hearts, we do not need to pretend.

The bigger challenge is for believers to respond to God in trust and praise during their season of lament. There is always a weakening of our faith when we feel compelled to lament our circumstance to God in prayer. That does not mean we do not have faith. Nor does it mean we do not trust God to save us from our predicament. This is why we have to preface any prayer of lament with words of praise.

Praise sets the atmosphere for worship. In Psalm 86, David is explicit in his petition to God for help. Whereas we are not sure about the circumstance that prompted him to write the Psalm, we know his need is urgent. Therefore, he laments his condition as he asks God to preserve his life (v. 2). David lavishes the Lord with praise and demonstrates a spirit of worship in the midst of his difficulty.

In the first 7 verses, David presents his condition, makes his petition, and reminds the Lord of his graciousness to those who love Him. Then he switches his focus to praising God for His Sovereignty. In the latter section of the Psalm, he affirms his trust in God as he beseeches the Lord to, *turn to me, and have mercy on me! Give Your strength to Your servant, And save the son of Your maidservant. Show me a sign for good, That those who hate me may see it and be ashamed, Because You, LORD, have helped me and comforted me* (v. 16-17).

QUESTIONS FOR SELF REFLECTION

PRAYER OF LAMENT

(Psalm 69)

What is a prayer of lament?

___

___

___

Why do people lament in prayer?

___

___

___

What are the emotions often expressed in a prayer of lament?

___

___

___

Why did David offer his lament in Psalm 69?

Have you ever prayed a prayer of lament? If so, how did you feel?

DAY 31

PRAYER OF MEDITATION

There are vast numbers of writings about meditation in Christianity and the religions of the East (Buddhism, Hinduism, etc.). Meditation, as a religious discipline consists of concentration and contemplation. During the concentration phase, the individual focuses their spirit for the purpose of connecting with the divine. Through contemplation, the individual beholds the light of God through the "eye of the soul."

Christian meditation prayer is different. It is scripture based. During meditation prayer, the supplicant meditates on the scriptures. In Psalm 119:15, the psalmist declares, *I meditate on your precepts and consider your ways*. God told Joshua, *Keep this Book of the Law always on your lips; meditate on it day and night, so that you may be careful to do everything written in it. Then you will be prosperous and successful* (Joshua 1:8).

Why does God invite us to commune with Him through meditation? During meditation we not only talk **to** God, we also talk **with** God. The ears of the soul are more apt to hear from God during meditation prayer. When we take the time to concentrate on the Word of God and contemplate on the spiritual messages it contains, our soul can hear from God more audibly, and our spirit can experience Him more meaningfully.

Meditation prayer is about listening to God. It is about refocusing the spirit so the soul can identify the voice of God from the cacophony of noise that clamors for our attention. When we meditate in prayer, we invite the Holy Spirit to come and guide our time of prayer.

The purpose of meditation prayer is not to empty the mind; nor is it to discipline the mind. It is to hear from God and to talk to Him with the heart. The psalmist says in Psalm 19:14, *May the words of my mouth and the meditation of my heart be acceptable in your sight, Lord, my Rock.* There is indeed as much dialogue taking place during meditation prayer as there is during other types of prayer. The only difference is, in meditation prayer the individual stays in silence and surrenders to the Holy Spirit. He or she is then invited to hear the dialogue between the Holy Spirit and the Father concerning him or her.

QUESTIONS FOR SELF REFLECTION

PRAYER OF MEDITATION

(Joshua 1:8)

What is meditation prayer?

____

____

____

What are the characteristics of meditation prayer?

____

____

____

What is the purpose of meditation prayer?

____

____

____

What is the difference between meditation prayer and meditation?

____

____

____

What are the benefits of contemplation?

____

____

____

DAY 32

MERCY PRAYER

Many Christians do not know much about mercy prayer. Although they might have used the word mercy in their prayer, they may not quite know when to pray the mercy prayer or what is the purpose of mercy prayer. Thankfully, the Bible contains many passages that speak to this most powerful type of prayer.

Lamentations 3:21 tells us that Divine mercy is God withholding His judgment against us because of His unfailing love. Grace is the daily provision and blessing we receive from God despite our sinfulness. Because of God's mercy, we are redeemed from eternal death and delivered from eternal judgment.

At one point or another, every Christian has prayed the mercy prayer knowingly or unknowingly. This prayer is often uttered in times of distress, or when a person feels contrite because of a sin committed. I use the mercy prayer to intercede for those who are dying of a terminal illness or the poor and downtrodden. Indeed, whenever there is a natural disaster, I pray the mercy prayer for the victims of the disaster. Moreover, when I am convicted by the Holy Spirit because of my disobedience or willful sin, I pray the mercy prayer.

The mercy prayer is a unique type of prayer with a central

emphasis on asking and receiving divine mercy. That need for divine mercy may not necessarily be the result of a sin committed. Our Eastern Orthodox brothers and sisters maintain the closer we get to God our need for mercy becomes more pronounced. "It's as if the cross awakens our appetite for His compassion. We actually desire God's mercy more, the closer we get to Him, not only because we see our shortcomings in light of His perfection but also because knowing God is knowing He is merciful."[1]

Many individuals pray the mercy prayer in the Bible. For example, when David prayed his mercy prayer in Psalm 51, he was not only looking for forgiveness, he wanted reconciliation and restoration. David highlights the holiness of God, and in his brokenness his appetite for the Holy Spirit was awakened. Thus, he beseeches the Lord not to take His Holy Spirit from him, and to restore in him the joy of His salvation.

Some people pray the mercy prayer when they are overwhelmed with guilt and shame. Others ask for relief in their distress (Psalm 4:1). Many individuals pray the mercy prayer to ask for healing when they are struggling with a major or terminal illness (Psalm 6:2). There are those who prayed the mercy prayer when they faced financial hardships or when they needed deliverance from attacks or persecution by their enemies (Psalm 9:13).

When we need help from the Lord to overcome the attacks of our spiritual enemy, we can cry out to Him for mercy from our persecutor (Psalm 28:2). When our weakness is greater than our strength, we have an open invitation to call on the mercy of God so we can overcome. Indeed the Lord invites us to, *come boldly unto the throne of grace, that we may obtain mercy, and find grace to help in time of need* (Hebrews 4:16).

---

1. Robert Gelinas, "*What is the Mercy Prayer*?" (Thomas Nelson: Nashville, 2013).

QUESTIONS FOR SELF REFLECTION

MERCY PRAYER

(Psalm 4:1; 6:2; 9:13; 28:2; Hebrews 4:16)

What is a mercy prayer?

____

____

____

When do Christians pray a mercy prayer?

____

____

____

What 3 things do we learn from David's mercy prayer in Psalm 51?

____

____

____

What are the benefits of praying a mercy prayer?

____

____

____

Why do Christians need divine mercy?

____

____

____

CONCLUSION

Knowing about the different types of prayer does not make one a prayer warrior. It only gives insight and helps to shape our prayer language when we go before the Almighty God in prayer. One of the reasons so many Christians struggle to cultivate an effectual prayer life is because they don't quite understand the dynamics of prayer as a spiritual discipline.

People who are in professional Christian ministry are obligated to know the different types of prayer so they can help others to pray more effectively. The way I see it, knowing about the different types of prayer is tantamount to knowing the different genres of writings in the Bible. Such understanding helps to provide a context for our prayer so they can be more relevant and effectual.

I keep going back to that brother who was invited to do an altar during the Sunday morning worship service. However, he proceeded to pray a prayer of intercession, supplication, lament, consecration and dedication, all at the same time. It took him over 45 minutes to say all of that, whereas he was only expected to do an altar call for about 10 minutes.

I saw a movie where a pastor was invited to bless the food during a wedding reception. This pastor went on to pray for God to curse anyone who would come against the couple. He petitioned God to give the couple many children. He prayed for God to resolve conflict between the two families etc., etc. Many of the guests were surprised and offended.

These types of things happen all too often in real life because people do not know when to pray a particular type of prayer. Many people think all prayers are the same. Are all conversations with one's spouse the same, for example? There are times when I use romantic language to serenade my wife. At other times, we come together for a more serious conversation about our future and the future of our children. There are times when we lament the way we treat one another in our conversation. It would be a mistake for any husband to start talking about romance when the wife wants to talk about financial security, for example.

Since prayer is our primary mode of communication with the Lord, we need to be mindful of when to use the right type of prayer. Otherwise, we are setting ourselves up for disappointment and frustration. What makes a prayer effectual is the awareness of the supplicant about the specific goal of their talk with God.

SMALL GROUP DISCUSSION

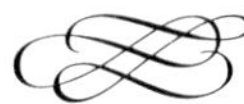

THE DIFFERENT TYPES OF PRAYER

The Question: What are the different types of prayer?
The Point: We can pray more effectively when we know what type of prayer we should pray.

Background Passage: 2 Chronicles 7:1-22
Lesson Passage: 2 Chronicles 7:14
Memory Verse: 2 Chronicles 7:14

Introduction

Prayer is a learned language. Just as it takes time to become fluent in a second language, it also takes time to become fluent in the language of prayer. Some people do not like to pray because they do not know what to say during prayer. Knowing what type of prayer is required in different circumstances is even more difficult. Yet, it is important for believers to take the time to learn about the different types of prayer, so their prayer can be more relevant and effectual.

Chapter V of this book focuses on eight different types of prayer. Obviously, a believer does not have to know every type of prayer to become a prayer warrior. The point here is not for people to become experts in the different types of prayer. The goal is for believers to cultivate a life of prayer. I want believers to be as comfortable praying as they are talking to their best friend. Developing this type of intimacy with God takes intentionality and awareness. My hope is that prayer will become our first response and not our last resort.

Background/Context

2 CHRONICLES 7 CAPTURES THE ELABORATE CELEBRATION OF THE dedication of the temple by King Solomon. The celebration began with the prayer of Solomon. Upon the completion of Solomon's prayer, the fire of the Lord came down from Heaven and consumed the offerings. The extent of sacrifices presented to the Lord throughout that celebration was ostentatious and bountiful. While the Lord was obviously pleased with the sacrificial offerings, He appeared to Solomon at night to reveal to him the benefits of faithfulness to Him, and the curses for disobedience to His decrees and commands.

King Solomon and the people of Israel prayed different types of prayer during that dedication celebration. They offered prayers of faith, thanksgiving, worship, and dedication. King Solomon led the way with his prayer of dedication that began in 2 Chronicles 6:12-40. In 2 Chronicles 7:3, the Israelites offered prayer of thanksgiving as they worshipped the Lord with their faces to the ground.

Prayer is not a "one size fits all" type of activity. Different needs may require different type of prayer. The challenge is to know when to pray a specific type of prayer. Those who have acquired that skill tend to be more effectual in their prayer. The Bible teaches us the different type of prayer we should pray. It is imperative that we read it.

QUESTIONS FOR SMALL GROUP DISCUSSION

What are the different types of prayer?

___

___

___

What is a prayer of intercession?

___

___

___

What is a prayer of supplication?

___

___

___

What is a prayer of consecration?

___

___

___

What does it mean to pray in the Spirit?

___

___

___

PRAYER TIPS FOR THIS CHAPTER

Understand the different types of prayer and when they should be used. Identify a type of prayer that you are more prone to use, and think about why. Spend time using the different types of prayer throughout the next week, and write down your experience of using the different types of prayer. Think about how a comprehensive understanding of the different types of prayer can enhance your prayer life.

Life Application Questions?

1. How often do you use the prayer of faith?
2. Write down a list of people who you are interceding for. Why do you think it is important to intercede for others?
3. When are you more inclined to offer a prayer of thanksgiving?
4. How do you pray to God when you are going through a season of grief?

Sample Prayer

Oh Lord my God, You who discern the heart and mind of human beings. Please help me to prioritize my fellowship of prayer with You. May I not be so rigid in communing with You through prayer, as to squander the opportunity to be transformed by the power of your Spirit! Please give me the wisdom to discern the appropriate prayer to speak in my times of need.